Trevor,

Stay fearless!

Lisa

2018

Praise for Taking in Strays

"I thoroughly enjoyed Lisa's writing in her book, *Taking in Strays*. I have used some of Lisa's examples in the continuing education classes I teach. I particularly love the story of Luke–an older dog that Lisa found and took into her home. It took a while to gain Luke's trust, they had to be patient and not try to force his loyalty. His loyalty came from being given the freedom to trust in his own time. It is the same with people, we have to be patient and allow our employees and coworkers to have the freedom and flexibility to grown. The entire book is enjoyable and insightful."

-Diane Powers, AU, CIC
Education Director
Independent Insurance Agents of Arkansas

"Lisa's perspective differs from many so-called management gurus because it focuses on our shared basic humanity. She exhorts us first to be the best people we can be, then lead by example. In this era of bottom-line-driven management decisions, Lisa's management with a heart approach is a breath of fresh air."

-Laura Mazzuca Toops
Editor, *American Agent & Broker*

"...I'm telling all my friends about this book."

-KH
Amazon reviewer

"Leadership in our world is changing and this author takes very real and human experiences with pets and turns each encounter into lessons of leadership. We have always known that we can learn so much from the animal kingdom if we pay attention and here it is captured in a creative way that is easy to understand and yet allows us to ponder a bit. Excellent work."

-Michelle Newell
President and CEO of Innovative Edge Consulting, Inc

Taking In
Strays

Taking In *Strays*
Leadership Lessons from Unexpected Places

Lisa H. Harrington
CPCU, CRIS, CAM, AAI, AIAM, AAM, AIP

Taking In Strays: Leadership Lessons from Unexpected Places
by Lisa H. Harrington

Copyright © 2015 Lisa H. Harrington.
www.takinginstrays.com

Published by Plaid Publishing
Texas, USA
www.plaidforwomen.com

All rights reserved. No part of this book may be used or reproduced in any manner whatsoever without written permission except in the case of brief quotations in critical articles and reviews.

A very special thank you to Nora Chandler for the use of the photo of Caleb.

Library of Congress Control Number: 2015958104
ISBN: 978-0-9964650-2-1
1. Business 2. Leadership 3. Mentoring & Coaching 4. Pets

Second Edition

Printed in the United States of America

For my parents.

Table of Contents

FOREWORD .... *xiii*

INTRODUCTION: Why Speed and Leadership are at Odds .... *xv*

PART 1: FOR THE DOG PEOPLE

ANGEL: Communication – The Water Story 1

JAZZ: Focus & Protection – The AC Guy & the Day We Got Her 9

CALEB: Mystery, Maintenance, Reward – The Lost Years Plus 17

LUKE: Keep Learning - The Old Dog Who Learned New Tricks 25

ZEKE: Stay Close – The 65-pound Lap Dog 31

MISTY: Beauty - Form Follows Function 37

ABBY: Consequences – Trust and the Stairs 43

LAZARUS: Know When to Let Go – Destruction 49

TOBY: Surprise! Enjoy the Unexpected 53

Part 2: For the Cat People

    HANNA: Gratitude – The Barn Story   63

    YODA: Presence – He's Always There   69

    BUTTON: Persistence – Meow   73

    LUCY: Nurturing – The 11 Kittens   77

    JAKE: Rest – Don't Judge a Book   81

    SADIE: When to Quit: The Night She Came In   85

    PEARL: Beauty and Patience   91

Part 3: For Friends of Avians

    JOSIE: Survival and Adaptation – How Did She Live to be 20?   101

    NAPOLEON: Fearless Exploration – "Whattayadoin?"   105

Part 4: For the Cowboy in All of Us

    GABBY: Routine – Kindness Counts   113

    KENDALL ROSE: Acceptance – Being Home is Enough   121

Acknowledgments   cxxix

About the Author   cxxi

Foreword

WE'VE ALL BEEN TAUGHT about the importance of good leadership in business. We also know that there is a difference between leading and managing. How is it that so many "leaders" don't know how to lead? The answer is simple in my eyes. They don't know how to implement the lessons that appear in front of them every day. Even more though, you have to be open to learning from the lessons. Taking in Strays is a different kind of book on leadership. Using stories about animals and relating them to leadership principles is an ingenious method that Lisa Harrington chose. Most people learn through story telling and what better way to remember the lesson than through stories using animals as the catalyst! I found myself thinking of some of those opportunities that were presented to me that I wasn't even aware of, until I read and re-read *Taking in Strays*. Lisa's knack of relating her own stories to those situations in the business world is right on target. Another book on Leadership you ask? No, not another one.... THE only one you need to have as a reference guide. I highly recommend you read this book multiple times and share it with those you are bringing through the ranks as future leaders.

- *Judy Hoberman*
Author, *Selling in a Skirt*
& *Famous is Not Enough*

Introduction
Why Speed and Leadership are at Odds

Considering that the foundations of business success are time-honored, I often refer to Maslow's Pyramid in my speaking and consulting engagements. It has and continues to be one of the best tools for learning the practice of leadership. I believe that people can only respond to you based on where they are in that process; nothing I've seen in three decades changes that fact.

With science and technology, we can leap forward in huge chunks of time and space. I am a fan of Daniel Burrus, a man ahead of his time in this area. His predictions are not of the Nostradamus genre, but he has been correct more often than not about where our inventions, technology, and products will take us in the future. (Trekkies might say that he and Gene Roddenberry have a lot in common.) I love the contradiction in Burrus's philosophy about, "skipping the problem," and, "go opposite," along with other wonderful concepts, helping us train our minds to see solutions that are invisible when using traditional thinking.

However, in the realm of human studies, time is moving much more slowly. I am a student of the human condition, having worked with hundreds of employees and students over the years. With the disclaimer that I am not academically qualified in the social sciences or psychology, I want to make the argument that in our lifetime, human beings will not change very much. Humans have not changed very much at the basic core for a thousand years or more. We survive first. We think afterward. We love first and think later.

In other words, we can only see, hear, and focus on the level of the Maslow Pyramid in which we live. Within that set of circumstances – and not any further – we will exist until that layer is satisfied. Sometimes we work up and down this pyramid, depending on the stage of our life or current circumstances. Emotional reactions and decisions are the reality which leaders have to address in their own practices and among their charges, employees, or other team members. This thought might even explain gang warfare, religious wars, and – unfortunately – some politics!

Likewise, if we leaders can learn to understand the layer in which our employees live, we can direct our influence properly. We can deal with their needs and their next steps in development from a place where they can hear us and react in a progressive, productive way. Like it or not, if we don't address them from their own perspective, we will not be effective.

From a generational and cultural perspective, this also applies to the marketing we do to our customers. Kelly McDonald addresses this diversity issue in her terrific book *Marketing to People Not Like You*. And if you are in sales, you might find the answers to one of your diversity issues in Judy Hoberman's *Selling in a Skirt*.

Thousands of books have been written about how leaders should behave, coaching us about our actions, our processes, our methods. Fewer books exist which instruct us about how we should treat our charges, focusing on their needs and not ours. This is my message, and hopefully, this little book will help you see and adjust your leadership style from a new perspective.

The challenge of leading with a focus of others' needs is that we live in an era of split-second responses and life-like descriptions in 140 characters or less. Taking the time to individually relate and respond in person to each employee is going to feel like an impossible request. Getting to know people at that level takes time, which is arguably our most valuable and most guarded asset. Similar to a orchestra conductor learning the music he may never actually play, you are beholden to the process of actually knowing your charges; you cannot avoid it if you want to have the most effective team, whether that is your family, your staff, your volunteer group, or your business partners.

My story has always included a love of animals. Time,

XVII

space, geography, marital status, education, tragedy, and joy have always included the silver threads of my strong faith and my beloved pets. I can't remember a time when I didn't want a horse. Dogs were as much a part of my day growing up as they are now, and I cannot count the number of cats I've had over my several decades on earth. A few of the birds I've owned didn't make this text, but Marti Gras, Margarita, Coast, Goofy, and Charlie still left me with warm memories that I'd never trade.

Seemingly everyone has a story about a pet. A vast majority, 88 percent, of Americans own at least one pet, and 72 percent own two or more. Science tells us that humans live longer when they have a pet. (This is great for me; I've loved so many pets that it means I'll live forever. At the least, my arrival at the Pearly Gates will be met with a stampede!) Some studies tell us that stroking a cat or dog lowers your blood pressure; one report even claims cholesterol is lowered. Medical centers the world over allow therapy dogs. The reasons listed vary, but owning a dog might mean you walk more or further; and there are also benefits to owning a cat. The proof, at least according to the World Wide Web, goes on and on: keeping animals as pets is good for us! Besides, there's just something about keeping and caring for pets that makes humans more human.

Just as we treat each animal according to each's unique needs, leaders must be flexible and adapt their style to the needs of their charges as well. This book attempts to demonstrate that idea.

I have found that the most classic stories, told many times and in different ways, are often the purveyors of the most valuable lessons. Consequently, I thought it would be interesting to compare some fun tales about animals to the lessons I teach in my role as a manager, leader, speaker, and author. So wherever you are on the pyramid of human experience, I hope you will find and share the unexpected lessons of leadership in the pages that follow.

For the Dog People

Communication
The Water Story

ANGEL IS MY DOG, and as dog owners say, I am her person. She has spoken to me since the day we met, sometimes as clearly as if she could speak English. Of course, I don't mean this in a freakish, supernatural way. Somehow, I can look at her when she is "talking" to me and know what she means.

The first day I met Angel, I had volunteered at a vet clinic owned by my friend, Kris. I opened the clinic that morning and cleaned the cages of the few animals that were there. As I was caring for some cats, Angel was bouncing off the walls of her kennel at the prospect of someone to play with. She was tiny then, just 12 pounds or so, and was as white as a snow angel. I found out later that the clinic staff had already named her Angel.

"What's wrong with the little white dog?" I asked my friend.

"Oh, nothing," she said. "She just needs a home!" In a small, but wonderful way, her answer changed my life forever.

Coincidentally, I had just landed a great job running the education division of a large trade association, and within a week, my husband and I would be moving from Orlando to Tallahassee. We told Kris that if Angel hadn't been placed in a permanent home by the time we bought our new house, we would come back for her. Then, visiting her later that week, we said to hold her for us until we found a house. However, by the time we left–only six days after I met her–we decided to purchase a kennel and take Angel with us to live in the hotel.

Fast forward two years. One evening, I was sitting in the kitchen with my husband, Paul, and our friend, Millie.[1] We were engrossed in conversation and I was ignoring Angel. She started nose-butting us, one by one. Then she started barking. Then butting *and* barking. We all assumed she wanted to go outside, yet she wouldn't go when we opened the door. This continued for several minutes.

Angel's next move was noticeable and significant. She walked over to her water dish and forcefully planted both front feet on either side, dropped her head, and heaved out a very loud, dramatic sigh! The water dish was empty! She had told us over and over, but we hadn't listened. Instead of giving up,

---
[1] Name changed.

she used several different methods and tones, including body language, to make her point.

We learned that when Angel speaks, we should listen. To this day, she will come to get us when a cat is locked in a closet or when one of the other dogs is ready to come back in the house, when someone new is in the yard or when the bathtub is overflowing. And she makes it very clear when it is time for us to go to bed, ready or not!

ANGEL'S LESSON TO LEADERS is clear, isn't it? Communication sometimes requires that we try different methods, that we pay attention to our body language, and that we be attentive to our tone and words. Eventually, we need the other person to listen. Our responsibility as leaders is to be persistent until we have the attention of others and until they hear us. This is much more difficult than it sounds, but here are a few points to live by:

First of all, be a role model regarding the important skill of listening.

Ask yourself, "Do I demonstrate the active listening skills that my employees will need to use when I speak to them?" (We'll talk more about that later when we hear about Jazz.) **Then be a role model regarding the important skill of speaking.**

Ask yourself, "Am I building the right background for them? Am I starting in the middle of the story and assuming they know what I know?"

In preparing to communicate with others, respectfully get their attention. Ask if there is time to talk and be polite about your interruption. Better yet, ask for an appointment. (Isn't that what you'd ask of them if they needed you?) Then set the stage for the conversation. Give them the information you'll be discussing and be sure they have time to review it.

Next, follow the lessons taught in speech classes:
- Tell the audience what you're going to tell them
- Then tell them
- Then tell them what you've told them

In a similar way, use these guidelines when you're talking to someone about what you want them to remember or do for you.

As you begin your conversation, **present the information from their perspective. Start with why they should care.** You don't have to sell them on doing the job. You're the boss. You could bark out orders if you'd like, following up and looking over their shoulder, but this won't get you very far in the long run.

Be concise with your request. Take time to share details in an organized, logical fashion. This works even when you aren't making a formal presentation. Leave a few bread crumbs so they can see where you are going. Like Angel, use body language, tone of voice, and careful selection of your words to make your point.

Some time ago, UCLA did a study and found that only 7 percent (7%) of our message to others is understood due to the words we use, our verbal choices. Another 35 percent (35%) of our message to others is perceived via tone of voice, our vocal choices. A whopping 58 percent (58%) of our message is received via our body language, our visual choices. (Please note that I am using the word *choices* deliberately.)

Verbal = 7%, Vocal = 35% and Visual = 58%.

Tailor your message for the recipient. We can be sloppy with our language (verbal choices), or we can carefully decide how to phrase a sentence so that it can be received in the right way. Norman Vincent Peale has a great lesson on the positive use of words versus their negative use. I recommend that you read his work.

Learn to control your tone of voice and match it to the message you are trying to impart. Our vocal cues come from the tone of voice we use. If you haven't heard yourself on a recording, you should do so. How do you sound when you are upset or angry or happy? With Angel, she varies the tones of her bark and we've learned which ones are for a crisis, which are angst, and which are just her way of saying hello to the dog next door.

Body language conveys most of our message. It is critical to remember a few things when speaking with someone face to face: an aggressive stance or closed posture are visual cues, used since the hunter-gatherer days, that have kept a place within the deep recesses of our brains. We cannot ignore them. We can suppress our reaction, but they are still noted by our personal supercomputers at a primal level. Therefore, if you are attempting to communicate in a non-threatening way, use care with all three areas: verbal, vocal, and body language.

Here's an example: You are upset with a decision that an employee made, but you only want to coach him on the issue. You feel no need for reprimand because he is new to the company or unfamiliar with the area in question. You carefully choose your words, even using dulcet tones with a smile, yet you have an aggressive stance with your feet apart and your arms crossed. You are sending a very mixed message. By the same token, if you are too relaxed in your posture when there is a problem, you may not be taken seriously.

Begin carefully and build your message. One reason that using proper body language is so important is that, once a defensive barrier is in place by the recipient of your message, little can be accomplished. Therefore, even when discipline or more assertive conversation is warranted, you must tread carefully or the message will not be received: the barricade will go up and discussion of the subject will be difficult. You may waste a lot of time trying to climb over that defensive wall to make yourself heard. At worst, you can simply end the relationship or employment.

Much of the value of body language is lost by telephone conversations. Somehow, you must convey the sense of your authority, your openness, and your style in your tone of voice and choice of words. (This is why so many telephone communication experts emphasize smiling into the phone if you are a customer service professional.)

It's even worse with email. Now 100 percent of your message is carried by the medium that is only 7 percent effective. This is why email (along with texting, tweeting, and whatever comes next!) can cause so many problems for us. We may seem much more harsh in our communications than intended, and a smiley face can only do so much to help.

As basic as it seems, communication is important enough to warrant careful, detailed, and ongoing study. Nearly every author or expert in leadership and management talks about the value of communication.

Be consistent in your style of communication. If you tend to be abrupt one day and wordy the next, it will be harder for your charges to read your intent.

A great example of this is one boss who seemed to use the back door to the office when he was having a bad day but came in the front when he was feeling good about things. Everyone thought they had figured out his pattern.

"Don't bother him today," they'd whisper. "He came in the back."

However, it wasn't a true pattern. As a manager there, I mentioned it to him one day, and he was shocked. He asserted that he used the back door for completely random reasons, having nothing to do with the state of the company, his mood, or any of the reasons the employees had inferred.

In my own experience, because I'm generally an optimistic "morning person," I've been quietly asked if everything is okay when I've come into the office without a boisterous or chatty comment. With these examples in mind, you can see how non-verbal cues and inconsistency can cause issues quite by accident.

Remember: Verbal = 7%, Vocal = 35% and Visual = 58%.

Focus & Protection
The AC Guy & the Day We Got Her

JASMINE IS PAUL'S GIRL. Of course I love her, too, but generally speaking, she will stay in whatever room Paul is in, while Angel is rarely more than a few feet away from me when I am home.

The day we got Jazz was a tough one for me. We still had Misty, who was aging fast, and we had just lost Abby to a freak accident. She was a young dog that was supposed to be Angel's new playmate. We had waited about a month and then found out about a pet adoption expo where we thought we might find her a new playmate. The previous weekend, we'd been to the pet store and shared our story with a shelter volunteer.

"I have the perfect dog for you!" she said. "Please come back for the expo next Saturday and meet Jasmine."

When we entered the expo, my hubby went straight over

to the volunteer we had met and sat down with her and Jasmine, but I was overwhelmed because there were hundreds of dogs that needed help. I began to wander the rows of kennels and got lost in the enormity of the pet population. (Please, spay and neuter your pets!)

I made my way back to Paul, who had focused a little better than I. He immediately saw my confusion.

"Here, honey," he said. "Take Jasmine for a little walk." I took the leash of an adorable, five-month-old Border Collie mix and trotted her around the store. This dog never took her eyes off of me. By the time I got back to the volunteer desk, I knew she had found her forever home.

Jasmine still never takes her eyes off of me when Paul isn't home. At night, she cuddles in the bed for a while, but when we go to sleep, she lies on the floor, usually near the door. She is always in protection mode.

Once, the AC repair guy made the mistake of stepping too far past me into our house without my permission. Jazz brought him back to me with a little nip to his posterior. She didn't bite or break his skin, but she grabbed the back of his jeans. Like all herding dogs, she can make her point about which direction you should be going.

Our farrier in Tallahassee, a big strong guy who deals with 1,200-pound horses every day, wouldn't come through the gate the first time he saw Jazz–fur raised–on the other side, barking at him. She was only six months old, but she didn't know this person and she was waiting for mom or dad to say it was okay!

I feel pretty safe with this dog by my side.

JAZZ TAUGHT ME A few different lessons.

Keep your focus. Don't get so overwhelmed by the multitude of choices (or voices) that you forget your mission. We have so many choices now about many things. Did you know that there are hundreds of toothpaste brands? In our work, there are even more choices, but none more important than how we behave with our colleagues. We have the ability to be many things to many people. This is true both for the individual and for the collective.

As a leader, you have the responsibility to focus on many layers, but most importantly, maintain your own focus. When a staff member is speaking, are you really listening? Or are you trying to multi-task? Do you interrupt them to take a phone call? (Rude!) Is one eye on your email? Technically, in terms of brain function, we cannot multi-task. Inside our head we are actually bouncing from one thing back to the other over and over again. By doing this, our brain is up to 40% less effective, causing us to make more mistakes and potentially hurt someone's feelings.

Active listening may be one of the most difficult disciplines we have to practice. We have to look at our companion or employee and really focus on them. Pick your head up from the desk and put the phone, paper, or other distractions down. Simply look at them while they are speaking. Amazingly, this can be really difficult. For example, do you have a notification bell on your email, ringing every time there is a new message? Turn it off! You might even minimize all the screens on your computer to reduce further distraction.

Next, clear a space across your desk (if applicable) so that there is no implied barrier between the two of you. Close up files and move them aside. The body language you employ can also help: lean in and focus. Nod, smile, and gesture!

You can also use verbal cues to let the person know you are engaged in the conversation. "Oh?" and "Uh, huh?" are two of my favorite ways to get a person to keep talking. I learned this from my friend Bill. Keep your focus by asking questions and commenting on various aspects of the conversation, such as, "Wow, I bet that was hard to do!" or, "Great idea!" as you go along in the conversation.

This may seem rudimentary, but the most basic and important things we do are often the ones that get lost in the hurriedness of life. Unfortunately, we tend to ignore the polishing of these basic skills because they are assumed to be done naturally. We are born knowing how to hear but not how to listen, which takes skill and practice. Listening isn't the only focus you need.

Do you focus on your own set of needs, your own training, and your own time to think and process? Jazz knows the cool, dark corners of our home, and she finds them. Interestingly, she knows just where to lie so that if we move around the house, she can still see us. I have a home office and she lies down in the breakfast nook, right across from me. I can move into the kitchen, living room, or dining room without her having to take her eyes off of me. This allows her to rest and relax. Have you scheduled your own training time, your rest, and your time to think? Do you allow such time for your employees? In fact, do you insist upon them *taking* that time?

Focus your team. It's your responsibility to keep their eye on the ball, which takes a great deal of effort and requires several steps.

1. Do what must be done to have a up-to-date vision and mission statements, then create language around those mission that empowers your internal code. Standardize everything to the three or four core values and missions you develop. Don't just brand your product. Brand your mission. Virtually everything you do–internal documents, external news items, meeting agendas–can be organized or communicated around those concepts. This helps the ability to focus come very naturally, no longer requiring staff to listen to pontifications about the methodology. It helps create a habit. Even accountability is enhanced because everyone will know what direction they are going all the time. Day to day, your team can take a look up from the desk and check their activities against the vision, values, and mission statements of the organization to be sure they are using their time wisely.

2. Take care of each other. Vigorously protect those you lead, and help them not to damage themselves. Regarding the overused word, "empowerment," I like to say, "I will give you all the rope you need to hang yourself, but I will never let the trap door open below you." Don't let them work so hard they forget other priorities such as family and rest because no one wins when they are burnt out.

Most generally, your best employees need most of your attention. We have the bad habit of spending more time on our marginal employees, because we hope we can fix them. Unfortunately, this means we don't have time to develop the ones that actually deserve our time. Since we often allow the marginal employees to continue in their position way too long, we actually punish the good ones who end up carrying more than their share of the load. Because they are the good ones, they will continue to shoulder the load until they have deprived themselves of rest and refreshment. They may even burn out, which manifests in many forms: giving up, becoming ill due to lack of rest, or developing an attitude that suffers.

Keep track of the time you spend with each employee, which will keep you from falling into this trap. It is fine to spend time trying to bring poor employees into the fold with training, attention, or even trying different assignments, but be sure the ratios are right.

Help them stay focused on the bigger mission. Others may try pulling them away from the task, like Jasmine kept the

AC guy out of my house. Be sure you are aware of all the distractions that are in the way of the people you lead, even if this means eliminating or giving new life to processes that are old or unnecessary: there may be stale procedures that are just, "the way we have always done it." These can easily rob you of efficiency and effectiveness.

Technology can have this effect as well. As Maslow said, if all you have is a hammer, everything will look like a nail. Be sure your systems are current. This is difficult with the changes that come so fast, but the old rule of driving all work down to the most cost-effective solution still stands. Similarly, if you have someone doing work that can be automated (or delegated), you have inefficiency. This does more than affect the bottom-line. Your staff will be demoralized over time when they see the impact on their day simply because you won't make the investment. The topic of reward is an entirely different subject for another chapter, but for now, just remember that most folks want to do a great job, and you reward them by allowing them to do so when you provide the proper tools.

Jasmine's ability to focus on what matters and to protect those she loves has provided an endless number of lessons for me. I hope you'll receive these as your own and apply them as you can.

Caleb

Mystery, Maintenance, Reward
The Lost Years Plus

WE HAD JUST TWO elderly dogs left: Angel and Jazz. We thought we might even take a break between dogs once they passed. We had three full-time cats and one part-time cat that we babysat frequently. So we thought, why not give ourselves a break?

Caleb was a surprise. On the way home from the dentist one day, I found Caleb running around the main road a couple of blocks from my house. This was very dangerous for him, so I picked him up and put him in the car. He settled right in with me, as if he knew me already.

Calling the phone number on his tags revealed that he was in foster care, looking for permanent placement. As an escape artist, he'd already gotten loose from the foster mom three times. She had seen me pick him up; in fact, she was running after him.

By the time she could come pick him up, he'd met our other dogs, sniffed around a couple of the cats, and I was hooked. When the foster mom came by, I was surprised that she said I had to relinquish him. She said he'd go back to the vet and be crated because of his escape tendencies.

"I'll just keep him," I said. "Why make him go in the crate? I have a perfectly fine fenced yard!" (I thought I did, anyway. More on that later.) They did the inspection of my house and yard right then, gave me the info to expedite the adoption, and took him away.

"I'll just keep him," I said. "Why make him go in the crate? I have a perfectly fine fenced yard!" (I thought I did, anyway. More on that later.) They did the inspection of my house and yard right then, gave me the info to expedite the adoption, and we got him back a few days later.

Caleb is a mystery to everyone. He had a microchip, so we know someone loved him very much, but they had moved away or changed every known contact–email, phone, home address–and they had never updated the chip. We suspect that he ran off and they gave up, and then later moved away. We know exactly when he was born because the vet info on the chip was still good and they still had his file, but there was a five-year gap in data. When found, he was a mess. At eight pounds, he was only two-thirds the weight he should have been. He was matted, nearly blinded by all the hair, and very sick. He was very lucky to be alive after surviving on his own in the outdoors.

Once cleaned up and neutered, he went to foster care and on to me. And slowly, I see little hints of what his life might have been like. Loud noises cause scampering. He was terrified of the dark at first and knows how to find the little nooks and crannies in our house to hide himself.

He's a real lap dog, as he was bred to be as a BichPoo. If you are home, he is on, near, over, under, beside, or with you. And he's super smart, learning what we want and what our commands mean to him, so he is adjusting well. We're good owners and know what to do in these cases, so he's lucky (again) that I'd been on my way home that day. Somehow, I think he knows this and he's learned to trust us explicitly.

MANY TIMES, WE DON'T really know as leaders what our employees or other followers have been through in their lives. Their reactions to our leadership may be different than we expect because of their life experiences. It is our job to adjust our style and our reactions to their needs. We have to be chameleons.

Over time, we can glean glimpses into their lives and they can learn to trust us. This is a very important point. You cannot rush this. No amount of process, procedure, manuals, training, or money can change the past for our people. They are human beings who have learned somehow to survive. Take the time to get to know them.

The more you share your stories, though, the more they will voluntarily share theirs. You will be surprised at what you learn. Some questions are inappropriate to ask, and of course, you cannot take on the role of counselor. But, like we did for Caleb, you can be consistent in your approach, and you can be careful.

Simple kindness goes a long way. Ask how they are doing on a regular basis. Pay attention to the details of their lives that you hear in discussions around the office and follow up. If there is a new grandchild, ask to see pictures. If a daughter is getting married, find out about the wedding and send a gift. If a husband is in surgery or ill, insist they take the day or the week off, even if they don't have the time accrued. They aren't going to be productive anyway, and you can't buy that loyalty. The precedent you set won't hurt. In fact, when others see this, you build their loyalty, too, and if someone abuses it you can manage that as well.

Maintenance is super important. Caleb is a breed that needs regular grooming. Like Jazz, who gets too hot in the Texas summers and needs trimming, he needs his cute, curly hair trimmed and his eyes kept clear. He has no way to do this himself, and nature provides no solution at all. He was bred for this level of grooming. Unlike Jazz, who would have been fine if left in her native colder climates but was imported to warmer places, Caleb will always be 100% dependent on human intervention for his maintenance and care. So are your charges! They need you 100% of the time for maintaining their attitude, their trust, and their performance.

Do not confuse this with micromanagement. We're talking about maintenance, not oversight or looking over the shoulder of your folks all the time. And I'm not just talking about maintenance of their talents and strengths with training and development–that should be a given these days. **What I mean is maintenance of their trust in *you*.**

First of all, this is a very individual-oriented process. It's okay to study generations, cultures, demographics of various groups, and classes of humans and apply what you can when it works. But every single person is a completely unique entity. To really inspire performance, you have to know them personally and act or react accordingly when you are trying to bring out their best. If we taught Caleb the same way we taught Jazz, it wouldn't have worked. His reactions to various commands were motivated by completely different things. For example, the first thing we figured out with his training is that "stay" was familiar and he does it pretty well. Jazz was great with "sit" – Caleb, not so much. Only dried chicken strips and some serious persistence helped him understand that word.

What works with one employee may not ever work with another. They may be trying really hard and they may be doing their absolute best to understand, but you may not be speaking their language. Caleb wasn't really trying to escape, but the slats in the fence were so far apart that he didn't see them as a barrier, just a small door to walk right on through. He got away from our yard twice before we finished adding the smaller wire around the bottom to keep him in. His intent wasn't really to leave home, but we didn't provide the right message to him about his boundaries with that wide open fencing.

Individualize your rewards. Don't make the mistake of applying rewards the way you want them. Be sure the reward not only matches the value of the work performed, but the needs or desires of those you want earning it! If you are rewarding someone with money when they need more time with family, you are missing the boat. One dog wants a pat on the head in my house, and another wants a slice of cheese. It's real for us humans, too.

There is a famous cosmetics company that is a great illustration of this. They offer money, cars, jewelry, trips, and even ball gowns or luggage as ways to reward their folks. One pharmaceutical company gives out a catalog with hundreds of items and employees earn points to buy goodies from candy to cars. You can do this in many ways yourself. Small businesses can buy into a points catalog, too, or you can keep it simple and offer time off, movie tickets, longer lunches, and gift certificates to choice restaurants or local attractions.

Individualizing your rewards programs takes time, but it works. Just like Caleb can have more fun, looks so much cuter with regular trimming, and needs different cues about how to behave, your efforts to personalize your care of your charges will also pay off!

Keep Learning
The Old Dog Who Learned New Tricks

WHEN WE FOUND LUKE at our Walk to Emmaus church camp, he was clearly a dog who had been loved but lost. He was scared to death, but not emaciated yet. When I saw him lying on the door mat outside the conference room, he watched me but did not get up. I knelt down to his level and called, and he very cautiously approached and let me pet him.

Others at the camp had been feeding him that April weekend, but couldn't catch him. We figured that someone who had been in the RV park next door lost him and simply couldn't find him before they left. Luke let me hug him and pet him a while, then went back to his doormat. I asked my husband to please bring him home the next day if no one claimed him. Luke trusted us enough to get into Paul's truck. Interestingly, he obeyed a young woman at the camp, but not Paul. It took him a long time to trust men for some reason we'll never know. He did not have a microchip. We put up signs, but no one called. And, when we had him checked out at the vet, we cured him of a very serious case of heartworms.

Once we gained his trust, we never lost it. But we had to be patient. He was a loyal dog, too, fiercely protecting us against other dogs even in his old age. We always felt safe when Luke was around. All of our animals are rescues and, like Luke, I think they know we saved them.

TRUSTING YOUR PEOPLE ENOUGH to let go of the reins is tough. In difficult times, the usual management style is to hold tighter, get stricter, and allow less freedom. This is backward. In hard times, people want security, not a noose. In fact, the freedoms and flexibility that most crave and which the newer generations will value even more than money, are often a kindness that management can show to employees with no direct cost to the company.

Long-term results require long-term strategies. We measure ROI in so many ways that we try to measure everything in dollars and cents, which works fine for many areas of our work. However, some cannot be measured that way. Some long-term methods cause change to come in millimeters or in pennies.

Trust is one of those long-term strategies that will build people up slowly. It builds teams an inch at a time. It's also a solution that doesn't have to break the bank. Allow some remote work, an extra day off, or flexibility in the methods used to get the job done. Most employees want to do a good job. It's tough to let go because we've been burned by the small percentage that have taken advantage of us. We want tight reins to avoid that pain again. It *does* feel personal when that happens. In the end, though, that pulls us in the wrong direction. To get the horse to move left, you push with your right leg. It is not instinctive, but it works. When you show trust, you earn it. Take the chance!

The other thing about Luke that we could never quite "fix" is that he knew he was a DOG, and he was okay with that. Unlike any of our other animals, Luke was always okay with being a dog. For the most part, he slept on the floor, ate his own food, and carried himself like a dog. He never tried to be human as so many canines are prone to attempt.

Angel was indignant at the idea of being a dog. My aunt used to joke about her adopted beagle, Copper, and how long it took them to break him of all of these bad habits. "He won't come in the kitchen, or sleep in our bed, or cuddle on the couch," she'd say.

Luke was like that. He was unabashedly joyful about being a dog. He literally *leapt* with joy; he'd bounce and jump and sometimes quiver with the sheer joy of life. He didn't do that at first. The heartworms weren't discovered right away and while he was sick he was fairly quiet. But once he was healed, he was determined to make the most of his newfound energy. Luke was nine when we found him, past middle age, and he lived to be 14. And right up to the end, he bounced with joy every day.

One of the best ways to discover joy in the workplace is to utilize the best of your talent every day. This applies to you and to your staff. Unfortunately, more than half of the US population is in a job that never utilizes their best talent. In fact, some studies have shown that most Americans can't even name their best talents! *First, Break All the Rules* and *Now, Discover Your Strengths* are two of the best management texts on the planet and speak very directly to this point. To gain the most productivity from an employee means putting them on the right tasks suited to their own hard-wired best abilities. The books by Marcus Buckingham, et al explain carefully that experience and training are essential, but not the issue here. Proper placement based on natural talent will garner the best results. And more to my point is that, once properly assigned and working in an area of real talents where the results can only get better over time, employees can find joy in their work day.

Volunteer leadership proves this. Many people out there that are volunteering (some 30 million people in the U.S. do it) and getting more joy from that experience than from work. Why? Well, of course, part of it is the philanthropic nature of the work. Giving back provides its own reward. But the other part is that people naturally gravitate to that which they do well. The singers sing, the chefs bake, the math lovers do the books, the gardeners till. Look at any well-organized charity and you'll find joyful volunteers doing for free that which they should probably be doing to earn their living. They would be much more successful and probably happier if they did. **Ask your followers what they do as hobbies and charity work outside the office and you'll get a real insight into what they should be doing for you in the office.**

This isn't conjecture. The books I referenced come out of a Gallup Poll and scientific research. You can look around you and see it every day. Take the time to look in your own office or workplace!

Zeke

Stay Close
The 65-pound Lap Dog

ZEKE WAS A STUNNING creature right from the start. Even as an adult dog he looked exactly like a six-month-old full-bred German Shepherd. In reality, he was part Chow Chow, part Shepherd, part who-knows-what. But as a pup at 20 pounds or at his full weight of 65 pounds, he always looked like a puppy. He had the fluffy hair and rounded nose. His markings were visually striking and perfectly balanced.

Zeke came to us via a neighbor. Our friend was a teen who occasionally would dog-sit our other three dogs. She came to visit one day to tell me about this pup she found along the side of the road by a country lake where she was visiting.

"He was just sitting there," she said, "like he was waiting for something." But he was utterly alone and she could tell he had not eaten much. Puppy dumping is a shameful human behavior that happens all too often. So, having a gigantic heart, she took him into her truck, fleas and all, and brought him home.

She said even though she was feeding him on her porch, there was not a fence and her mom didn't want another house dog, especially since we could tell he'd get pretty big.

"Bring him over," I said. "I've got a great fence and we'll find him a home." I fed him and introduced him to the other pets. When Paul got home that day, he knew this dog would be his. We had four already. What was one more?

Our other dogs adapted quickly in the yard so we brought him inside. The first thing he did was find high ground: he got up onto the fireplace hearth, even though it was summer. He let out a big sigh and slept. Security and safety in our care must have seemed obvious to him. Minor attention from the veterinarian was needed for a type of dermatitis called mange, but otherwise he was a very healthy dog and he fit right in.

Zeke's favorite place in the world, even after he was 65 pounds, was in our laps. While he was a puppy we encouraged this, and snuggled with him on the couch every day. As he grew, this was more interesting to accomplish, but I'll never regret the times he sat right on my lap, snuggled up while we watched a movie together. We did not get nearly enough time with this precious dog.

One day at work I got a call from a neighbor.

"I'm so sorry to have to tell you by phone, Lisa, but I found

Zeke along our street. He's been hit by a car, I think, and he's gone."

I called Paul and rushed home. My neighbor had found him about a block away, but had lovingly brought him to our driveway and covered him with a tarp. I'll never forget that act of kindness. Once we brought him inside the fence and buried him, we started trying to figure out how he had gotten out. At that time, all of our dogs would stay outside all day while we were at work. We were in Florida, so weather usually permitted this. They were spoiled, with two dog houses and a huge porch with a dog door and toys, food, and water up there on the porch. So we couldn't figure out what happened! Had someone let him out by accident?

After a thorough search of the fence line (back then we had five fully fenced acres, so this took a little while), we found one of the side gates open. The latch was broken and the only thing we could figure is that Zeke had jumped up against the gate while chasing a squirrel or something and had knocked it open. Then, he must have been chasing a car or truck or maybe even another squirrel when he was hit.

Now, this is the hard part, which I never understood. Why did the person that hit him just keep driving? His tags had our phone number. Even an anonymous call would have been the civil thing to do after they killed our dog. There are some things I'll never understand about humans, and I've been studying human behavior my whole life.

THIS SAD STORY TEACHES us a few things. First, love while you can. Never, ever assume that there will always be tomorrow to pet your dog, kiss your spouse, or read a bedtime story to your kids. Sad, bad, shocking, sudden, terrible things happen. You'll want those great memories if anything does. And even better, if you live long, happy lives because you are generous with your time and your love, you'll have lost nothing and gained everything.

Zeke also taught us about joy, fun, and staying close. At work, this may seem frivolous. We've discussed the need for joy and structured play in the workplace. Management science now tells us that having fun at work is a guarantee that your people will be more productive.

How do we stay close in the workplace without crossing boundaries of inappropriate fraternization? How do we get to know someone without getting to know them *too* much and causing even the perception of bias, or worse? One way to do this is to balance your time with employees very carefully. Zeke sat on my lap as much as he did Paul's. He was generous with his time for both of us. We liked to say the Zeke "wallered" on us. He'd crawl up there and roll around to get settled. If Paul and I were sitting side by side, he'd stretch out across both of us.

Another way to look at this could be to reflect on something my Grandma Jean used to tell us. She was an ELCA pastor's wife for 40 years. While at church, she seemed to be friends with everyone. I used to marvel at her ability to move through the crowd and work the room. She always remembered names, faces, and families. She chatted them up and then, when she was done, she went home alone with Granddad. She did not socialize with the parishioners after church unless it was a church function. Now, she may have even carried it a little too far because I know she was a little lonely. But she'd say, "I'm the preacher's wife, honey. I can't have favorites. I love them all the same, like God does."

This may be the way you can handle the concept of staying close to your staff the right way. Be aware of the time you spend with each one, and don't play favorites. If you have lunch with one person all the time, even if it is just because of convenient scheduling or because you both like Chinese food or you're working through projects together, there will be a perception by the rest of the staff that you're friends with that person first, boss second. Have lunch or breaks with everyone, randomly. You don't need to keep a scorecard, but pay attention.

Why should it matter? What harm is there if we make friends with other managers? And what do I mean by "everyone" here? Aren't we supposed to avoid the line staff and not fraternize?

It matters because you can't lead someone you don't know.

It's impossible to inspire or to gain trust if you don't take time to know them. And there is no harm in being friends with *everyone* at the office while at the office. Fraternization implies that you are spending inappropriate time with a subordinate outside of the office. But while at work, take the time at breaks or lunch to talk to everyone who reports to you, and everyone who reports to them. Get down at least one level below you on the organizational chart, if not further. You should recognize them in the hallway. You should sit in the kitchen and visit over coffee enough that you know all the faces and all the names and most of the names of their children and families. Dare I say it? Sometimes you might even get caught actually making the coffee and surprise a few folks about your level of participation in normal things. I'm sometimes amazed at the perception of administrative staff and the way they put management on such a pedestal. They can't reach you if you stay up there.

So stay close. In every economic situation, you need to hang on to your best people. How do you know who the best are without knowing them? And, if you pay attention, you may know when there is a little shift in their behavior that could alert you in advance that they are restless, dissatisfied, or ready for the next phase of their career. Why make them move to the next company or job? You could see it well enough in advance to talk to them about it, share an opportunity (or create one for them), and demonstrate to all your valuable staff that opportunities do come for hard workers. After all, actions speak louder than words.

Misty

Beauty
Form Follows Function

MISTY WAS THE ONLY purebred dog we have had, but she was still a rescue of sorts. One of the attractions between my husband and I was our love of dogs. "You've gotta have a dog," he said to me when we were dating. And so, as soon as we got engaged, we decided to get a dog.

It was easy. We mentioned to a few friends our desire for a great pet, and our choirmaster knew someone who was retiring a Weimaraner. I didn't even know what that breed looked like; at the time, I wasn't a student of dog breeds. So we went to the home where Misty had been born and raised to meet her owner. She cautioned us that Misty was a bit shy. In fact, she'd been retired a little bit early from shows because she got camera shy from all the flash cameras. She'd won a few blue ribbons, had her two litters, and now needed a place to live out her golden years.

We were asked to sit down because of Misty's shy nature. Imagine the owner's surprise when this cautious dog walked into the room and straight up to Paul, putting her head immediately in his lap.

"Well," she said, "I guess she's picked her new owner!"

Misty was absolutely gorgeous. She was a classic cinnamon Weim with amazing light-colored eyes. She was lithe and spectacular to watch in motion. She was a little shy after all, but not with us. After a few weeks at our house as our only pet at first, she got used to the frequent visitors and would probably have led anyone to the good silver. While in our first house, we got a good routine going: she got a two mile walk from mom every morning and dad took her to the pond to toss the ball every night. It was an awesome set up.

FORM FOLLOWS FUNCTION. Misty was bred to be beautiful. Smarts weren't a big requirement, but a gentle disposition and an obedient nature were imperative in the show dog world. Misty helps us see that **we need to balance how something looks with what it is supposed to accomplish.** So when you are working with staff, you must realize that appearances count. Perception is everything. Impressions are made, and you can't take back a first impression.

There's a lot to consider in this. Let's start at the beginning. When an applicant (or customer) walks into your office, what do they see? How long has it been since you've really looked at the environment around you at work? Don't take the attitude that if it's functioning there's no need to upgrade. It's easy to think that taking care of the outward appearance of your space is frivolous or a waste of money. You might think, "We don't get walk-in retail trade, so why bother?" But humans are nesting creatures, too. We create a certain type of space around us and each person has a different need. Otherwise we wouldn't have so many types of homes, so many decorators, or such a wide variety of architectural wonders and styles throughout the centuries.

So, while you need to be sure your office space has function, it should also look nice. Form follows function, so first be sure you can get the operational requirements set up and then go for style and comfort. This will also affect employee productivity.

Form counts after an applicant is hired. Just how well do you handle orientation for your new staff? This is so easy to dismiss. What do they really know about your firm, its vision, mission, customers, or industry? Taking the time to teach them can feel like a waste because you can't tie any direct return on investment to this time you spend.

Think again about Misty for a minute. She won a blue ribbon or two in local and state shows. She didn't do that by herself. Hundreds of years of breeding, careful diet and exercise, and scores of hours of training all went into those wins. We spend the time and effort on sales training so much more easily. I have taught hundreds of sales people in my career and that check is always so much easier for the client to write, because in theory, the sales results can be measured and ROI assigned. Consider all support training to be a part of the sales process. Or consider support and administration as a part of customer retention. Whatever you do, don't neglect it. All sales people are more productive with the right support.

Then you can look at orientation as the beginning of all training for all staff. This is the place to get everyone on the same page. Do not fail here. That first impression sets the stage for a lifetime! What your employees think about you and say about your firm in their public and private lives can be affected by that first couple of weeks in your office. They are your voice, officially or unofficially.

Finally, Misty taught us about play. Our first few days with her, we thought it would be good to keep her in a smaller environment when we were at work. This technique is common with new dogs to help them feel safe during transition to a new home. It went so well the first week. We had a large crate for her, and while that was left open and optional, we did keep her in one of the smaller guest rooms when we weren't in the house. It was Misty's room and her food, water, and toys were all there for her, as well as a nice, comfy futon to lay on if she didn't want to be in the crate. We figured as den animals, this was probably more comforting to her and she would learn about the rest of the house whenever we were home.

One day the second week, though, we came home to a completely shredded newspaper and a few teeth marks on the wooden arms of the futon in her room. Misty had a ball tearing up that paper, we could tell. She was bouncy and happy when we got home. It was too late to scold her (you only have about five seconds after the fact to discipline a dog, or they have no idea why you are mad). But we couldn't figure out why she did it. Was she lonely? Was she upset? No! We realized we'd forgotten to put her favorite toy in the room with her before we left for work. She just found a substitute toy to entertain herself for the day!

If left unattended with nothing to do, most humans will also figure out something to pass the time. Either you provide positive experiences, assignments, or activities, or you risk that your charges will find negative ones. They might find the good stuff, but they might not. So, that water-cooler gossip who is causing all the trouble may need to be fired, but he may just need to get better direction, and he definitely needs a lot more to do to pass the time. When too busy working, he won't go looking for any trouble to cause.

What does this have to do with play? Two things: first, be sure your employees have the opportunity in a safe, channeled way to socialize. They are going to do it, right? We know that humans are meant to congregate in groups. So provide a structured outlet for that basic human trait. Let them play together in such a way that you know it's positive, and you can even use that time occasionally to teach a lesson or do some team building. Don't dominate every staff luncheon that way, though, or it will start to feel like work.

The second thing about play is that somehow, part of each day should feel playful, or some part of each person's job should feel fun. This is easier said than done, but if you properly place your employees in jobs that fit their talents, they shouldn't feel like every day is a grind all day long. There should be parts of the day that feel fun. And you can create a great sense of that by your example as their leader. Are you having fun? Do they know it?

Abby

Consequences
Trust and the Stairs

ONE THING ALWAYS LEADS to another. Our first dog, Misty, was getting older and had a spinal condition that was keeping her on the porch more and in the yard less. Some days, we let her stay in the house when we were gone. This meant, though, that Angel had to stay in or be alone in the yard. As a young dog, Angel still had a lot of energy to burn and she was a runner who wanted open spaces. A favorite memory of Angel is her running around the outside of the house, going so fast she seemed almost flat.

Anyway, with Misty getting older we knew we'd need a companion for Angel pretty soon.

About that same time, a couple of house sparrows built a nest up in the rafters of the porch. We loved this and enjoyed having their special music to hear when we were sitting on the swing. One early Saturday morning while having coffee on the swing, I realized there wasn't any music. I looked around and found not one, but both parents dead on the porch. When I got closer to the nest, I realized the babies were crying, making that special chirp when they need to be fed.

We figured out that the parents had flown into the ceiling fan! We were devastated, and that afternoon Paul began the work to screen in the porch.

Meanwhile, we needed to get the babies to the animal rescue organization. We pulled down the nest and took them to the only open vet's office that could transport them. While we were there, we noticed they had several kennels of fostered dogs. Since we knew Angel would need a companion soon, we went to take a look.

Abby was part Basenji, so she didn't bark much. She was adorable with red hair and only weighed about 30 pounds. She was so shy, and almost cowered in the cage. When the clinic let her out and brought her to us, she rolled onto her back immediately. They suspected she'd been badly abused based on her behavior and her condition when she was found. We knew we could give her a better life.

So, home she went. Angel had a new best friend, and things went along swimmingly until we realized she refused to go up the stairs to the second floor. It wasn't a big deal, since most of our time was spent downstairs anyway. But we wondered why and asked the vet. The answer was, "Probably that was the abuse. Someone tossed her down a set of stairs." So we took our time and carried her, trembling, up and down those stairs for weeks so she would know it was safe with us. Problem solved.

WOULDN'T IT BE NICE if we could give and receive trust as easily with our employees? If we could just carry them around a bit and they would trust us?

Receiving trust usually entails the reverse. That is, you have to trust them first. There are several areas to consider in trying to prove your trustworthiness to them.

First, just talk to them. This plays back to the discussions we have had about learning who they are and getting to know them. You have to share some of yourself as well. Trust is earned, and not easily given to strangers.

So you have to reveal a little of yourself, too. Open up a little at a time about your own life and job, and through sharing you'll find they open up a bit to you as well.

When they do, you can begin to understand their situation. You can find out what their dreams are, or what parts of work are most difficult for them or where they live in the Maslow Pyramid, for example. If you haven't read up on Maslow, it's well worth it.

As you begin to see their perspective, you'll find ways to help them, share your experience, or give a little guidance on their career. The time you take to do these things proves you to be more than a boss, and someone who they can turn to when they need help.

Remember, they can't focus on work if they have issues elsewhere in the pyramid. Even though you can't get involved personally, you can arrange an employee assistance plan, perhaps through health insurance or other means, to be sure that your employees have what they need in all areas of their lives. This is common in many cultures around the world, but surprisingly, with all our progress, we miss it in many small and medium-sized businesses in the USA.

Once you trust each other, you can scale mountains (or staircases) together.

Abby's second lesson was one of consequences, and one thing leading to another. Helping the birds helped us to find her. On a lesser scale it pushed us to screen in the porch, which had many pleasant outcomes.

Abby was only with us for 11 months. We won't ever really know what happened, but on a Memorial Day Friday night we came home and found her in the yard, already deceased. We have some theories, but we didn't bother with an autopsy or struggle with "why" because we knew she'd known love and real family for the last part of her short life, and we believe we'll see her again!

That led us to Jazz, who lived to be 13 and was a dear part of our family that we'd never have known if not for that sad Friday. Every action has its consequence.

Your actions every day are watched by your staff. Every action has a consequence. When you are confused, angry, lost, or even hurt by your bosses, take care to keep your game face on. During a particularly unsettled time in my career, I was given this simple but life-changing advice from Melissa, one of my charges. She simply but firmly said, "You're our leader. Lead us!"

Leaders do not have the luxury of allowing their own personal emotional baggage to show publicly. Deal with that, get help if you need it, but never do it in front of your team or group.

I like to think of leaders as conductors of a grand orchestra because there seem to be so many similarities to the difficulties and rewards of our work.

A conductor may never play the instruments, but they must know how to read the music. They have to get the very best individual efforts from each member, but those efforts must be coordinated to maximize the benefits from and for each. And, they can't just focus on perfection of style or hours practiced. The coordination of effort has to include playing the right music from the right section of the piece because if the brass section play perfectly and the strings are exactly in tune but are playing from two separate sheets of different music, the result can be very ugly. And if the conductor is out of sorts and isn't keeping everyone on the same beat, all that practice can go to waste.

It's a little like that for us as leaders. If we are out of sorts and miss a beat, so does everyone else. One or two bad days can destroy the delicate trust we've built up with our charges, even if we are unaware we are having that effect. They are watching all the time and we must be vigilant about managing their perceptions. If we'd tripped down the stairs while carrying Abby, she might relive her abuse and we might never get her up those stairs again, even though it was accidental.

We need to be vigilant about caring for ourselves. We absolutely must stay physically and mentally healthy. We are responsible for so many lives. They count on us to be at our best.

Like the birds leading to Abby who led to Jazz, our actions will always have a domino effect. Set the example. Lead!

Know When to Let Go
Destruction

SOME RELATIONSHIPS JUST AREN'T going to work. Ever. And if you are really lucky or very observant, you can figure this out early and avoid the kind of destruction I experienced in one short 76-hour period.

When my friend the vet heard that I wanted a dog (before we got the horse), she started keeping her eyes and ears open for an adoption for me. I was single again and thought it would be nice to have a little more company than just the birds. One Saturday afternoon, she called me to the clinic where she was working and I met a beautiful Boxer mix who seemed perfect. He was smaller, docile, and so gentle. He almost seemed timid. He'd responded well to his bath and was very excited when the leash went on and we got in the car. We got home and played, walked around the block, and got to know my house. I didn't have any dog beds purchased yet, but he didn't mind. He jumped right up on my bed with me and settled in for the night. We both slept just fine.

Sundays I usually went to see Grandma at the nursing home nearby. I wanted her to meet the new dog, so we went to my house to have lunch. When we got there, I noticed Lazarus had pulled down one of the vertical blinds (easily reattached) and one of our doorknobs was scratched up. We didn't mind and had a wonderful day with him. He even came back to the nursing home when I took Grandma back and visited with the residents; they loved him.

The next day I made a mistake, though. Instead of leaving him out on our nice screened porch for the day, I put him in a large kennel inside one of the bedrooms and closed the door. How was I to know he had severe claustrophobia and separation anxiety?

It was too long of a day for his first day alone, and I'll caution you, too, to ease your pets into the new routine. By the time I got home, he'd managed to rip the plastic section of the crate, tear down every blind in my house, eat the entire bottom half of the bedroom door where he was, crush every door knob in the house, and chew through the moldings and drywall to the insulation at the front door trying to leave the building. He was, amazingly, only mildly raw in his mouth from the efforts. Generally, he was unharmed.

When I walked in the house through the back, I couldn't

see the damage until I turned the corner. He saw me, whined once, and flopped over on his side. He let out this huge sigh of relief and went immediately to sleep. He'd knocked over Josie's birdcage in the process. So I called him out to the porch and tried hard to stay calm while I tried to find Josie. At first I was too loud and scary, but when I calmed down she chirped once and I found her, amazingly unharmed. She had just a little scratch or two.

Lazarus ran off, jumping through a hole in the porch screen that I thought was too small for him. I called my friend the vet and she came by to collect him. Another friend came over with a shovel and a wheelbarrow – that was how much destruction he'd amassed.

There was nothing I could do for this poor boy. While I hope to this day that the vet could find him a nice, big place where he could live outside (maybe under someone's farmhouse porch), there was no way I could cure him of such a strong terror of being alone. I had to cut the cord. Immediately. It was almost ironic that I'd named him Lazarus. Our relationship died so quickly, but I hope a better situation was resurrected somewhere else.

Unlike Sadie's story, when we talked about how you should make the decision for yourself to move on, Lazarus shows that you may need to cut the cord with someone else.

Most states allow a 90-day trial period of some kind with employees. Please, take advantage of that. Look hard and carefully, and if it isn't working, stop while you are ahead and let go. This is very, very difficult. We want to give everyone the best benefit of the doubt, and good leaders often feel responsible when they have hired poorly. You are, indeed, responsible. But you can fix the problem quickly and minimize the impact on your bottom line and on your staff morale.

First of all, you waste money on time and training if you allow a poor hire to continue. That's just a practical reality. More importantly, you spend too much time trying to fix the problem, often not realizing that you are neglecting the high-quality employees that need your attention. This is backward. Spend more time with the folks who are getting the job done and less on the ones who are never going to get it.

In the end, the waste and pain of stopping sooner instead of later will always be best for everyone.

Toby

SURPRISE!
Enjoy the Unexpected

TOBY WAS A REALLY fun surprise. After Angel passed at the age of 16, and after the first edition of this book was already published, it took me a long time to be ready for another dog.

We lost four pets in about 16 months (Jazz, Button, Angel and Gabby). When it was clear we'd also lose Hanna very soon, we started talking about what we wanted to do next. Would we be okay with just one dog and one cat? I wasn't sure I'd ever want another dog, frankly. Angel was very special to me, and I still miss her today. But Paul was ready after six months or so, and I just couldn't say no to him. I have lost count of the times he said "Sure!" when I've wanted to bring home another pet. At least once, with Pearl, I didn't even ask first. I owed him this.

We'd done considerable research over the prior year or so,

and found a wonderful organization called DASH Dog in Dallas that was specializing in fostering and placing herding dogs. Their main breed was Australian Shepherd, and we wanted a small or miniature female. We thought around 35-40 pounds would be perfect since that was just slightly smaller than Angel. Plus, my aunt, cousin and a co-worker all had Aussies, all female, and were always talking about how they were the "perfect" dog for us.

That Sunday, when Paul said he was ready, I got online at DASH Dog and filled out the application. We got an email back in about 20 minutes! Okay, maybe it was a couple of hours, but it was really fast. One of the staff of the shelter said they would love to show us some female miniature Aussies.

"We have a really special Aussie mix dog that we think would be just perfect for your situation. Would you consider meeting him as well?"

Of course, she emailed a picture of the little guy and he is amazingly beautiful. He has perfect brindle markings and a naturally docked tail like most Aussies. Paul and I talked a few minutes and decided to meet him. We asked a bunch of questions, because we've had experience with both male and female dogs and wanted to be sure he'd be a good fit. We had such great advice from a prior rescue group (with Jazz) that we decided to take their advice. We didn't even look at other dogs. That Thursday, we went to meet him, and we took Caleb along.

It was a match. Caleb sniffed him a few times and laid down. Avery just sat and was very docile. They were, at that time, about the same size. We renamed him Toby, partially in honor of the woman, Tobi, who had been fostering him, and partially because I like the biblical name Tobias. Tobi figured he'd top out at 45 pounds, and had fostered him for about a month so knew how calm and quiet he was for an Aussie.

And that was it! We took him home and started to get him acclimated to the place. As he was a puppy, we decided we'd use the extra-large crate and get him used to our house for a few weeks before allowing him to run around. We strongly believe in crate training dogs because there are times when it's in their best interest. The crate should always be large enough for the dog to stand up, stretch, and turn completely around. And, please, never leave a dog in a crate more than a few hours, or without a water bottle. I digress.

Toby absolutely loves his crate. He learned to go in there easily, and doesn't mind it. He goes in to sleep even when we are home and the door is open. After a couple of days we checked him out at the vet and got our first surprise.

"He's 5 months old and 24 pounds. Great dog," they say. "He'll be around 55-60 pounds fully grown."

Wait! Sixty pounds? Oh, well. Maybe he really isn't a miniature Aussie mix, but he gains weight so fast we aren't sure anymore. Let's find out, I think. We can do a DNA test for $60 and can be better owners to this dog if we know his heritage.

So what did we have?

Australian? Check!

Herding dog? Check!

Australian Shepherd? No!

It turns out he is mainly Great Pyrenees and Australian Cattle Dog!

Now, here's the weird part: the only other breed mentioned in the DNA test is Bichon Frise. You may remember Caleb is Bichon Frise/Poodle. So back to the vet we go, this time at his six month birthday to be neutered. I talk to her about the DNA.

"Could it be contaminated by Caleb's DNA somehow?"

"I don't think so," she says. "There would be two complete DNA strands and they would have probably asked you to do it again. Do you want a follow up blood test?"

Well, by now you may have figured it out. This dog is going to be very large. Great Pyrenees can weigh 120 pounds. Australian Cattle dogs, also known as Blue Heelers, are in the 35-50 range. Bichons top out at 15. So what do we have here?

After a lot of research on the Great Pyrenees, we're pretty sure that's his dominate type. His behavior and facial structure are really leaning that direction. At 10 months old he's still on track for about 60 pounds (thank goodness for that small Bichon in his blood!) and we are just in love with him. Everyone who meets him is smitten. We only care about his background because it means we can train him properly, and watch for health issues known to his dominate breeds.

Dog breeds matter because every breed needs different care and sometimes very specific training. You cannot train a Pyr the way you can an Aussie. Their motivations are different.

And the Pyr is incredibly independent, so you need to be very sure about what you want them to learn, and convey that confidence to them. They don't mind being the alpha dog. If you don't take that role firmly then they will, and with a dog that large it can cause problems. They are also much more protective than Aussies, since that's one of the traits they were intentionally bred to have. So handling a repairman coming into the house is different than with other dogs, for example.

TOBY HAS TAUGHT ME a lot. First, that most surprises are good ones! He's a little harder to train, but still gets it in his own time. He's so much fun, and he loves us unreservedly. Like Zeke, he still thinks he is a lap dog, although sometimes he sort of stands on his head on the couch. He's a bit of a clown. Like the Aussie we were expecting, he has more energy than most dogs, and needs serious exercise. Our single challenge is convincing him that Pearl the cat doesn't want to be chased. She's helping us teach him that, and–eventually–they are going to be great friends.

But this wonderful surprise is a lesson in paying attention, and being ready for anything. By doing our research, we are able to help him be the best dog he can possibly be. We know that he'll take longer to train, so we aren't frustrated. If we'd continued to expect him to react like an Aussie, it would be confusing and harder on all of us, but knowing his background means we have different expectations. He has been a model student at training classes and has been recommended as a therapy dog because he's so gentle. We may just try that.

In leadership, this teaches many things. As a leader, you will be surprised frequently. That much you already knew! You'll have people who aren't reacting the way you expect them to react. Be familiar with their backgrounds, and ask a lot of questions to be sure you're teaching, leading, and coaching in a style that works for them. You can't just lead everyone the same way and expect the best result, or even similar results. There are lots of ways to do this, the best being to simply talk to them as you go. You can study books, such as *Soar with your Strengths* or *Strengths Finders* or others.

Some people will be motivated by money, and others by time off, or attention, or public recognition. It's the leader's role to figure his out. And when you are coaching, you may find that some employees want to have time to read up on a topic before you visit, and some need the follow up documentation. A few will need both. Remember the basics of learning styles in humans, too: Auditory types like to hear, the kinesthetic need hands on learning, and most people are visual learners. Everyone learns best with some combination of the three.

You'll want to be sure to set expectations based on the reality of who you have on the team. It's not as simple as a cut and dried process in every case. I'm known for using the phrase "Standardize and scale!" when I'm working on projects and products at IRMI, where I am currently the Vice President. Even with marketing collateral you may have heard the idea of COPE: Create Once. Publish Everywhere. I love that sort of efficiency model. But it doesn't work with people. People (and dogs) can't be standardized! You shouldn't even want to do that. Learn what motivates each one, and what they need, and how they communicate.

It is your obligation as the leader to be the chameleon who makes the necessary adjustments to your own behavior, and to the assignments you give so that they match what your folks need the most. Don't ask someone to do something day in and day out that is not natural for them. It happens sometimes, of course, that we have to do things outside our comfort zone, but if that's all we get to do all day long then the stress will add up in negative ways. People want to do well, and they do best the things that fit their natural talents.

One of the traits of a Pyr is the paw. They literally want to hold you, have a paw on you, and will wrap their paw around your arm or knee. Toby is very gentle about this gesture. He's still a clumsy puppy many days, but when we wants that love, he just puts the paw up on you. If I had the expectation to train that out of him, we'd both be frustrated. But knowing the trait, I can treat it appropriately and we both get what we need.

When an employee has a particular trait that you don't understand, a phrase that they use a lot, or a tendency to act a certain way, pay attention. Try to find out what's behind it. Nervous gestures are also something to note. If you can tell when someone is starting to be stressed, you can head that off, or create an outlet for them. Stress builds up in small ways, and oftentimes, a number of small stresses can be harder on our bodies than one large one, because we try to dismiss them. Watch for the signs and learn what each individual needs from you to be most productive.

So after the shock wore off we have found our big surprise to be an amazing and loving addition to our lives. By taking it in stride, evaluating the situation, doing a little research, and with a little patience, we have learned how best to welcome him into our little family, and we are thrilled!

Sometimes, the surprises you get in life are much better than the plans you laid for yourself. Take time to enjoy them.

Sarah is another surprise. Just a few months after we got Toby we realized that the balance was still off in our house. Being so young and active, Toby needed a running mate.

Around the time we were thinking about this, the home of the executive director of the amazing rescue organization where we got him burned down. We responded quickly with the offer to help by taking in a foster dog. In a few days Sarah showed up in our lives. We fell in love, and so did Toby. Sarah brings a spark of joy that we will have forever. We failed as fosters and she is staying with us!

Pearl the cat is doing fine, although she isn't quite so enamored, but that's another story.

For Cat People

Hanna

GRATITUDE
The Barn Story

HANNA IS PROBABLY THE prettiest cat I've ever seen. She's delicate, very small, and made of rich, gray velvet. But good luck touching her. She's very skittish and she had to learn the hard way that if you want attention, you have to give attention.

We had her for a few months, and she was almost fully grown, but she simply never came out of hiding. This was before we had the cat door, and Sadie was already our barn cat at the time. Jake just itched to go outside, and sneaked out a lot. We were okay with that since he could always take refuge with Sadie in the barn. But Hanna was aloof to the point of me finally deciding not to bother. She was just never interested in being with us.

We decided to move her to the barn. She didn't seem to

care anyway, and she'd have her brother and Sadie for some company.

Turns out she didn't know how good she had it. And neither did I.

She was outside just a couple of weeks and we never saw her the entire time. Jake didn't really want to live out there after all, even though he liked to sneak out for a romp now and again. He hid in a corner of the barn and it was clear he was afraid, so we brought him back in. Jake outgrew that fear later and loved being outside.

But Hanna was nowhere to be seen! We hadn't seen her for even a minute since we'd set them up in the barn, and I was getting scared. What if a coyote had gotten her? Had she wandered off? Why did I make her go out there? I was beside myself.

My husband rigged the cat door to allow them all into the barn, but not back out. It worked! The very next day, he went out to feed the horses and there Hanna was, trapped in the feed room and very happy to have him pick her up and bring her inside to me.

I was ecstatic. She was skinny, but okay! And I learned an incredibly important lesson that day. She wasn't aloof at all. She was terrified. I had misread her signals completely. So, from then on, we used a very gentle way with her and she loved sitting on my lap any time. Although, I'll admit that, after Caleb arrived, it was a couple of months before she knew it was okay to share my lap with him. Again, she was fearful and cautious, and I allowed her to take her time to learn the new normal.

Once she was inside, one of my two-legged strays learned that she liked her head pet a certain way and she taught us that. Little details helped her learn to trust us. Then, we found out that she felt safe on our dining room chairs, so we would set her down on them. She was also afraid of heights, so Paul's 6'6" is really scary. He didn't carry her on his shoulder, but at his waist.

ALL THESE THINGS HAVE helped her to trust us–there it is again–and now she wants to be with us. She's our example for you of the one who has real crisis in their lives–the rape victim, or the abused wife–who you may or may not be able to help. This is a real phenomenon. One in seven people are alcoholics. Three in ten women are abused. As many as one in five children have grown up with inadequate nourishment, either because of neglect or poverty. The list goes on. Some problems are well beyond your realm and the best you can do is be sure every employee knows about the programs you have in place to help them, through an Employee Assistance Program or your insurance plans.

Measured approaches, kindness, and long-term thinking are what you need with these folks. Do not try to take on what a professional should handle here. There are liability issues and you might see them shrink away the way Hanna did when we put her outside.

The other lesson is less serious. She realized how good she had it inside once she'd seen what outside looks like! Many employees and employers like to grouse about how awful their company or their job is. But until you've seen the other side, you may not realize how good your life is. This works in personal life as well.

Take care with employees who have been in your office for many years. This grass-must-be-greener syndrome is common with them. They may need to volunteer for charity work or even be loaned to other companies to see how the rest of the work world lives. News articles about cuts, layoffs, reduced benefits, etc. can be shared to help your folks see that you are one of the good ones when it comes to employers. Simply opening someone's eyes is often all it takes to bring out the more positive response you want from them.

The final lesson here is to always cut out the cancer. Even though I read it wrong in Hanna's case, the basic concept must be explored: if someone isn't responding as they should and they are spreading poor attitude and ill will around your office, get rid of them, and immediately. Remove them from the scene so they don't poison the well. And make sure that in the culture you generate no one gets away with bad behavior.

Sometimes this means firing them. Sometimes, it means that they will have to sit in another department for a long time and be exposed to a different kind of work or structure to appreciate the one they have. And, like Hanna, they may come back with a new attitude.

Sometimes, that change helps them see they were in the wrong seat all along, and so they find a new place to live in their career or work life, and everyone will benefit with this change.

Your responsibility as a leader is to keep the positive flow of conversations, energy, and communication going, even if it means removing someone who blocks that for others.

Yoda

Presence
He's Always There

DON'T TELL THE OTHERS, but Yoda is my favorite of the cats. It isn't really that I care more about him than the others. I have just known him the longest.

His mama is Lucy. I found Lucy one cool February evening on the way home from choir practice. She was a very pregnant stray. On Easter morning, she had 11 beautiful, all-black kittens. Yes, I said 11! It is so rare to see a litter that size that even our veterinarian was surprised.

Yoda was the runt. A week after they were born I had to travel for work, which is a common part of my career. When I returned home, my mother-in-law asked me immediately to check on the kittens. "Something is wrong with one of them," she said. "He is not growing." She was right. I believe that Yoda was hours away from death that day. He was not with the litter. He was tottering away from them, barely staggering, and so tiny. I picked him up and his skin was all I could feel between my hand and his bones. He was starving!

I had her hold him and ran downstairs to the kitchen. I got a little milk to room temperature in the microwave and grabbed a needle-less syringe. You keep these things around when you have as many animals as we did over the years. When I got upstairs, I drew 3 CCs of the milk and put the tip in his mouth. We didn't even need to press the plunger. He sucked that milk down and would not let go! After 3 CCs more he fell asleep in my hand.

I fed him three times a day for a couple of months. I supplemented a few others who were too thin as well. With 11 kittens and only eight teats, poor Lucy never got a break. After a while, all eleven would run to me when I came in the room, crawling up my jeans hoping for a snack. It was quite a sight, me standing there with 11 critters hanging all over my clothing!

My cats are generally indoor-outdoor. Except right after a move, when they need time to acclimate, they have their own little kitty door to come and go as they please. Yoda loves this. In fact, when we have occasionally had to lock the door to the in-only position, he immediately figures out how to get out anyway.

I like to compare Yoda to mercury. He only tries to get away if you hold on too tight. He loves to have you pet him, just don't try to use two hands. Paul plays chase the light with him every evening. But if you want to catch him, good luck! Unless it's his idea or he's just waking up from a nap, he hates to be held, even for a minute, and chasing him is a lost cause.

This is not a reflection of his love for us. Yoda is always there. When I come home from work, he is in the house within minutes. I don't always see him right away, but I know he is there by the sound of the cat door flap. If I call him, he will always come inside. He gives me the honor of letting me know he is home by yowling loudly some nights, to say hello, or just letting me see him walk by. Sometimes, he comes though the living room and jumps up to rub our feet with his head.

You only touch Yoda on his terms. Once you know those terms, it is no problem, and he is a warm and loving pet. I can hold him and he'll allow it because I do it on his terms! Many nights Paul will ask if I have seen him that day. The answer is always, "Yes, he is right here," under the bed or behind the couch or behind the bedroom door. He is my cat. He always lets me see him.

YODA BRINGS MANY LESSONS, but the most important one is to simply be present. As leaders, we may feel obligated to always do something with or for our staff. Often, they just need to know we are there. A simple walk through the office every day to say hello may be enough. The open door alone is not adequate. Let them know you are there and available. Your most important work is to be there for them.

Some would argue that a leader's job is to work on the financials, or the strategic plan, or the development of the products that are sold, but whatever your title is, your main responsibility as a leader is to your people. So you must start there. Be present for them. The rest of your duties will come naturally after being present. You may even find you have more help getting those other tasks done!

Yoda also teaches us to come to the people in our lives on their terms. Everyone isn't like you. In fact, if you have risen to the level of management to be reading this book (or desire the advancement), then the vast majority is not like you–they cannot be. True leadership is a calling. So we need to be flexible in our approach, and able to adjust to the needs of the staff members individually. There is no cookie cutter application. Learn how each person will respond and reach out on their terms, not yours. When you figure out how to approach them in ways that make sense to them, you'll find they will be more responsive. Your communication will flow more easily. Contrary to popular belief, adjustments to behavior and approach must be made by you, not by your charges. That's the responsibility you accept when you become a leader. If you can do this, everyone benefits.

Button

Persistence
Meow

BUTTON IS A REALLY special part of our lives. First, he represents a real persistence when it comes to survival. My brother and his wife adopted him because he was a feral cat outside her office. He wasn't well-liked by her boss, so instead of letting him end up in a cat trap she took him home. He wasn't used to being inside, so he lived outside in their yard, coming inside to eat and hang out on top of the refrigerator when he wanted attention.

When my brother passed away, there were three house cats that his wife was taking with her when she moved back to her mom's. But, taking an outside cat from Florida to a cold climate in the Northwest wasn't a great idea, and she had enough to deal with already. So I took Button home with me after the funeral. He adjusted pretty well to the new routine.

All I can say for this cat is that he gets what he wants by sheer persistence. He would make Calvin Coolidge proud. His meow is well-timed, and loud. He is determined to be heard.

How persistent are you with your folks? Are you teaching this trait to them? Button borders on the obnoxious with his whining and meowing, but he is heard. You should find a way to teach your employees not to give up, no matter what the circumstances, until they are sure they have exhausted every option.

Sometimes we feel too pushy, so we stop trying. Or, we can't see any end in sight to the work involved in what we need to accomplish, so we come up with an excuse to stop. Button knows to give up when I leave the house, but he doesn't quit easily if I am home.

Button doesn't get what he wants all the time, or he'd weigh twice what he should. He tries hard to convince me he is always hungry, but he's only hungry for chicken or milk or canned cat food. The dry, healthy food dish is always full, always available, but he would rather eat the junk. (What human among us doesn't understand this, too?)

WE HAVE TO KNOW when to say NO even if our workers are being persistent about a request that we know is not appropriate or could even be harmful to our company, the mission, or the employee himself.

Our mission is to protect the ship, the overall health of the organization, no matter what that means. We are like the captain who would have to throw someone overboard, but in a much less dramatic way. We have to say NO and be unpopular sometimes, for their own good. Sound like parenting? It is. There's no generational issue here, we'll have to be a parent sometimes to Boomers the same way we might for Generation Y or others. It's just part of being the boss.

In my own experience, the need to be liked nearly took over my need to be respected, and it had the potential to derail my leadership career. It's a natural human tendency, stronger in some than in others, to want everyone around us to be our friend. That simply isn't possible if you are to be a great leader.

Wait a minute! Didn't I just say you had to share your stories, build trust, and get people talking to you in order to lead well? Yes. I meant that, too. But earning the respect and trust of your employees isn't the same as being their friend or allowing one person's desires to overshadow the health of the organization.

It's a myth that you can never be a friend to a subordinate, but you must be very careful if you do because you and they have to be able to handle it very well. You have to know when the friendship must come second for the good of the organization. It doesn't mean you aren't a friend any longer, it just means that you have to make your judgment based on the bigger picture.

My personal value statement is, "I strive to be a friend first, to live in the truth, and to serve graciously." But that doesn't mean I will put a friendship above larger responsibilities.

For example: as a friend to someone at work, you might share minimal information with them 10 minutes before a big meeting where they will learn that their own job is affected. You won't tell them details or break any confidence, but you might help them brace themselves. Your decision not to spill the beans in advance will be for the good of the whole, but your friendship means you'll help them through it if needed.

Sometimes you have to suspend a friendship. If you have to let someone go, it's appropriate not to contact them outside the workplace for a bit afterward, perhaps. Waiting for the dust to settle before you start meeting them for bowling again may the best thing for everyone. But you could probably still send a birthday card or call to say Merry Christmas.

Button knew we loved him even when he didn't get an extra helping of chicken, or when we got a dog named Caleb who stole his place in the bed with us at night. He loved his routine, and he came back to it eventually. History, trust, and consistency prevail.

Lucy

Nurturing
The 11 Kittens

I LOVE LUCY'S STORY. It was one of the most fun times in our household. Paul's mom was staying with us at the time, a couple of years after we moved to Tallahassee. I was coming home from choir practice one cold February night. We didn't get ice and snow much there, but this night was frosty. I saw a black cat sitting alone at the end of our dirt road and thought it was my black cat, Jake (or Blackie, my brother's cat). I pulled over and picked her up, and as soon as I did she just melted into my shoulder. The relief was palpable. I got in the car and drove the half mile to our driveway.

Once home, I took her to the barn and pulled out a little cat food. Sadie was staying out there at that point, so we had it stocked. In less than a minute, Lucy ate two packets of Tender

Vittles. It looked like she unhinged her jaw to take in as much as she could as fast as possible. I put the flea/wormer drops on her and turned on the little heating pad we kept out there in the big crate. Then I noticed how big her belly was. Oh, boy. Starving and pregnant. I had found her just in time.

We locked her in the barn overnight and brought her inside the next day, set her up on the second floor and expected kittens any minute. She was huge. We thought for sure we'd have March babies, but it was April before she had them. She was big like that for a reason. She had 11 kittens! What a wonderful adventure that was!

NURTURING IS A NATURAL instinct for most people as well. It's a behavior that we need to polish up soon as managers. Our world is about to change.

The Boomers are going to be gone from the workplace very soon. Nurturing the new folks in the workplace will be a part of every manager's life. Consider the new graduating classes in the past couple of years. According to sources at IIABA's InVEST, the graduating class of 2009 was the largest class ever in U.S. recorded history. Similar numbers are being reported for 2010 and 2011. So, as a kind leader, you'll need to nurture those young minds in a way that will be completely foreign to most of us Boomers and Xers. There is no need to repeat the mantras and methods that are so abundant on the topic of generational differences.

Being kind and nurturing to those young people is the first step to tapping all the wonderful potential that they have. All the communication and understanding of the generational differences will go right out the door if kindness is not part of the mix. As grandma used to say, "A little kindness goes a long way."

Nurturing isn't only about kindness, though. Sometimes it's discipline and training, and making the decisions that are right for someone when they can't do it themselves.

Lucy died of breast cancer many years after taking care of all those kitties. Her sweet nature will be remembered.

Rest
Don't Judge a Book

JAKE WAS ONE OF five black cats we've had. He was adopted along with Hanna. They may have been brother and sister but the lady who'd rescued them from the woods didn't really know.

Jake was playful and fun, and ran hard. We nearly lost him once because of a mistake giving medications (user error), but he recovered and became our linebacker because he got really big. I mean, this cat was huge. You'd never believe how fast he was. He didn't like being outside when he was young, but it wasn't long until he was eating most of his meals outside. He was our mouser.

He was, along with Sadie, the best mouser we ever had. On a farm, you want cats. It's really important. If you don't have cats, you get mice. Along with mice come snakes. It's dangerous not to have cats. So Jake was a hero for us and you could tell by his size that he was really good at it.

We literally lost Jake when he was about nine. He went out one day and we simply never saw him again, despite weeks of searching. We think there was a bobcat in the neighborhood that he just couldn't outrun. Normally, his speed and agility were a surprise every time you'd witness them because of his size. He couldn't run a long distance that quickly, but over the short runs he could fly.

ALL OF THAT SIZE was muscle. This was one fit cat. And one of his lessons to us is don't judge a book by its cover.

You have employees or colleagues who may seem quiet, or slow, or uninterested in their work. Challenge the premise. They may be like Jake and have amazing abilities you just can't see until you put them in a situation where they can shine.

Analyze what they do. Is the work you see good, but just slow? Are they in the right job for their abilities? Do you know what their true talents are or are they in the job because they were promoted past their own competence? I've had to clean up that issue more times than I care to say, by the way. The Peter Principal is alive and well. Check out the work of Laurence J. Peter and Raymond Hull in their 1969 book *The Peter Principle*.

Talk to them. Remember, not everyone can articulate what

they want out of life or a career. Some have to see it to explain. Some have never had the chance to experience anything that brought them out of their shell, or put a little razzmatazz in their day. You can't describe what you haven't seen without a lot of help. (Read Helen Keller. It can be done, but it's not easy.)

So, as the leader, it's your responsibility to be sure you are using the fullest, best talents of everyone in your organization. That takes time and patience, kind of like stalking a mouse. You have to wait and watch, and then really move quickly when you see what you need from someone. Talk to them about it as if they are having a really productive and positive experience. We've talked about joy (see Luke) and why it's such an important part of everyone's day when you are trying to achieve a positive bottom line.

Institutional knowledge is also important. It is very likely you can move nearly all of your non-productive staff into the right chairs and get that wonderful talent to come out and play, like Jake's ability with hunting. And when it's time to give up (see Lazarus), you should move quickly, too.

Jake's second lesson to us had to do with rest. He played hard, worked hard hunting, and when he rested he did it in style. Paul and I would be on the couch, watching something on TV or a movie. I'd look down and realize that Jake had, ever so gently, crawled up on my lap and cradled himself in my left arm. And he'd be out cold. That gentleness coming into my lap was one of the fun surprises with a cat that large. It was a routine for him. For an hour or two every night, he got that nap with me. It's what I miss most about him even today. So there was some routine there (also see Josie) and he really rested hard.

We don't rest enough in this country. It's an overused message, but still true. Technology makes it even harder to do. We go camping with our computers and smart phones. We take our tablets to the pool. We never really, truly, turn it off.

Jake's habit of really, truly resting every day worked for him. He also slept a good part of the day, of course, as most cats will do. But he had a set routine that was his time to refresh, shut it down, and completely crash. When he was on my arm that way, he was a limp lump of black fur. He even snored (so did Yoda; you could hear him in the next room).

The message to us as leaders is not only to rest ourselves (as the airlines say: put your own mask on first, then help others) but to be sure our employees have that opportunity. It's a good thing to have a requirement that employees take five days off in a row. Plan accordingly and don't demand that they keep their phones on! Leadership means we are responsible for the entire ship, and a tired crew makes mistakes.

If you are overworking any members of the crew, yourself included, you can't physically be at your best. This is really hard advice to follow in a world where seven seconds is too long for a web page to load and we describe our lives in 140 characters or less.

Leaders have to make the hard choices. We have to make very difficult decisions. One of the hardest is to simply stop and rest.

When to Quit
The Night She Came In

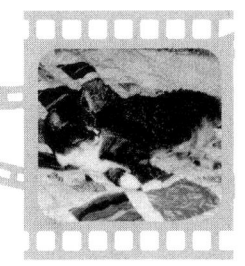

SADIE WAS NOT MY cat. She belonged to my brother, Al, who had to let me keep her when he joined the Navy (at 33, but that's another story!). He found her when she was just a few weeks old, crying under a bush near his apartment in Florida. She wasn't ours. But we loved her, and I think she came to love us, too.

Sadie loved the fact that she had five acres to run. Al had a porch at his apartment, but that was the extent of her freedom. When she came to us, we kept her inside for a short while, as you're supposed to so they get to know the new home. Then, she wanted very little to do with our house. She stayed outside so much that we set her up with a cat door, a big kennel, and food and water in the tack room! Her boy Blackie was with us, too, and lived with her outside. He didn't stay with us. Blackie went on walkabout two months after we got him and ended up staying in a neighborhood across the street. Cats are known for having a mind of their own.

Back to Sadie. For many years she lived in that barn. She and Jake were fabulous mousers. She survived a raccoon attack and two weeks in our bedroom with tubes and antibiotics. Then she was right back outside through her cat door. She knew she could come in the house anytime, and she did visit. But most of my time with Sadie was each morning and each evening when I went to the barn to feed the horses. She always came over to visit me then, and we had a routine. I think she wanted to check up on me regularly, and we had a set pattern to our visits.

One day after a trip out of town for a few days, I went to the barn and couldn't find her. I called and called, and had no luck. I was really worried. When Paul got home, I asked him if he'd seen her and he said, "She came inside the other night. Let's look upstairs." Sure enough, she was upstairs in the same room she'd recovered in earlier. There was always food and a litter box up there. She'd taken up residence in that room!

Paul related that my first night out of town he'd seen her streak by faster than he'd ever seen her run, and she went straight upstairs. From what we could tell, she never went outside again. We never did figure out what made her want to live inside, but something very clearly told her it was time to become a house cat.

ONE LESSON FROM SADIE Sadie is having a solid "management by walking around" (MBWA) routine. This way, you'll know when something is wrong so you can address it. The first time she didn't come to visit me when feeding the horses, I knew we may have a problem. If we hadn't found her and treated the infection from the raccoon, she wouldn't have survived. You can and should know your followers well enough to spot trouble. Walk around. Get to know them. Be a part of their everyday, even if just for a little while. Be sure you have enough layers in your management that each supervisor can know their own team well, but not so many layers that you don't know anyone. Create enough routine in everyone's day that you are all in tune with each other. Listen, observe, and react when needed. Don't ignore an issue until it's a full blown disaster. It's your job to rock the boat if it means keeping it from running over a waterfall.

This story tells us about one of the two hardest decisions that we'll discuss in this volume. One of them has to do with when to finally let an employee go. (See Lazarus.) But Sadie's story was about knowing when to quit, when to retire, when to move on from one company to the next or from one project to another. When is it time for you to leave, rest, retire, or just go lead a different team? How do we know when it's time to hang 'em up?

First, know yourself! Measure your joy each day. Figure out when you're reluctant to get going, when you are dragging yourself in to the office. Is it a phase, or are you done? Do you hang on well past the point of value because it's routine? Is your job easy for you, like "shooting fish in a barrel"? If there aren't enough ways to keep growing your talents and you can't find new angles at your current position to keep you happy and focused, you will drag down the rest of the team. Either invent something new to do within your job scope or get out. Sounds harsh, but one way to know it's right is to honestly measure the level of excitement you feel within when you are thinking about your next move. A little fear is normal with any change. Beyond that, are you doodling about your new plans during the current job's meetings? Are you thinking of the name of your book? Are you outlining organizational charts for your own imaginary company? Might be time for a change!

This thinking applies to project terminations, too. When is it time to cut your losses on a particular project that just can't get off the ground? Can something be shelved so resources can be used somewhere else, even temporarily? Is it time to kill the sacred cow in your shop?

Next, know your company and its people. Where do you rank in terms of value to them? Have you stagnated? Are you really leading anymore or just pulling the train cars down the same track every day?

Finally, know your industry. Do you work for the last of the buggy whip manufacturers? Are the leaders above you working in reality or just riding the wave of the current trend?

Sadie knew when to hang 'em up. Remember, you always want to quit while you're ahead. It leaves better memories of you for everyone, and you'll have more fun later in your new adventure!

Beauty and Patience

THE MOMENT I SAW Pearl's face on the rescue group's Facebook post, I knew she was mine. For most of my adult life I'd been considering a Calico cat. I hadn't ever actively sought one out, but I always knew that someday I'd have one. Most of our pets came to us, one way or the other. There have only been a couple that we've gone out to find.

That day, as soon as I saw the post, I made a comment online that she had her forever home first, then I picked up the phone and called the foster mama. Turns out Pearl had been living at a golf course near Whitney, Texas for a year or so. And, she was about to have her second set of babies, before she was even two years old herself. The woman that was helping her worked at the golf course, and knew her well.

"She's very friendly; and she loves a belly rub!" I was told.

And sandwiches. Even though they kept cat food and water in the cart barn for her, she loved it when the caddies shared their sandwiches. (To this day she comes running if she smells mayonnaise.) We'd only been in Texas a couple of years at this point. I hadn't realized the rescue mom was a couple of hours away and worried about how to connect before the kittens came.

"No problem!" she said. "We'll bring Pearl to you!"

Now I knew it was meant to be. Maybe it was time to call my hubby and let him know that we were adding to the family.

Pearl came to our house in Southlake on a Sunday, and late Tuesday night we had six adorable kittens. We knew the routine (six was a breeze compared to Lucy's eleven) and so we were ready. That evening, before they showed up, she had been out in the living room with us and for the first time curled up in Paul's lap. We were hooked, as usual.

Pearl was a wonderful mom. Her patience with the kittens and willingness to be stuck in that bedroom for a few weeks was very sweet. We had it all set up for her and felt it was safer than her trying to navigate with Angel and Jazz around. They were sweet dogs but there was no reason to take a chance of an accident. So, for six weeks she lived in the largest of our guest rooms, and taught her babies well. She had them partially weaned in about three weeks because we put soft food in once a day. She pushed them out of the crate when it was time for them to start exploring. And she taught them to play, climbing up the new cat condo for exercise and recreation. We found a home for one of the kittens with a friend, and the rest went (along with a large donation) to the marvelous Operation Kindness no kill shelter in our area. It being Christmas season by then, the kittens had a quick turnaround to permanent homes.

Pearl has gorgeous, crisp markings. Between her shoulder blades there is a large "paw print." And her face is split in the middle, right down her nose, tortoise on one side and black on the other. Her bottom and the underside of her tail make it look like she sat down in black paint. Her eyes are bright and a beautiful shade of amber that almost matches her tortoise fur. Her white dominates, and it's a gorgeous pearly white. You might think that is why I named her Pearl, and that's partly true. But when I found her, it was so sudden and unexpected I thought of the parable in the book of Matthew about the merchant who found a pearl so fine he sold all that he had in order to obtain it. It's a comparison to the Kingdom of Heaven. I didn't have to do anything that extreme, of course, but I did have that strong sense that she belonged with us, there was no doubt at all in my mind that she was worth the effort.

And she has been! After we let the last kitten go, it took her awhile to figure things out. When the weather allowed, we started letting her go outside a bit. Our cats have always been allowed in our yard during the day, and since we came to Texas we bring them in and lock the cat door at night. She loved that freedom, but I noticed she never leaves the fenced back yard. Somehow, she knows it's safer in than out. We have no doubt that she dodged a coyote or two on that golf course. We had to learn patience with her to gain her trust. It was months before she sat on our laps again after that night right before she had the kittens.

She was worth it. She is worth the time and patience it took to train her to come when called. Ironically, we discovered by accident that she will come when I sing to her. I sing in the church choir and, as I was rehearsing one afternoon, I happened to be out on the back deck, and she came streaking across the backyard! At first, I didn't understand why she came over to me. But after this happened a few times we tested to find out. She liked singing, and the higher the notes the better. (I admit to having a bit of a Snow White complex for a short time.) Eventually, she decided that she'd come in just by hearing us call her name, too. Now, at 9:00 p.m. we don't even have to go out and get her. She brings herself inside and puts herself to bed!

I also found that it was worth the time to train her that it was okay to share mom's lap with Caleb. She wanted that attention after a few months, but wasn't really sure about that curly haired dog in my lap. Finally, one day she crawled down over my shoulder and onto the lap, sort of laying on top of Caleb. She's incredibly special, and I think she knows that she is truly home.

She also surprised us with the patience she showed when we brought Toby home. That's a funny story, and he's a wonderful dog. He was barely six months old when we brought him home. And, he was quite a handful. He's a herding dog, and they are made up of energy and speed. So, as a puppy with that instinct, he decided that he should use Pearl for herding practice. He tried hard to get her to play along. In the first couple of weeks, we were afraid she was going to smack him with a paw full of open claws and take off half his nose.

He chases her around the house even now. He tried the puppy "please play" position, front legs down and butt high in the air, and the "doggy dance" going side to side in front of her and even the "spin" going round and round trying to get her attention. She watched, and stayed just out of his reach. Most of the time, she seemed bemused. Occasionally, she had just enough and swiped him hard with no claws. She punches and smacks and never hurts him. Somehow, this patient former mom knew that he was just a puppy, and really just wanted to play. And, unlike Caleb, who is older, and, well, not a cat, she never got flattened by his sheer exuberance trying to run across the yard. Caleb learned to duck and feint too, it just took him a little longer. Fortunately, he's already low to the ground and just rolled over those couple of times Toby couldn't put on the brakes fast enough to stop.

Pearl just knew that he wasn't a threat, and there is a calmness, even serenity to her approach with Toby. She'll sit on the floor in front of him and watch, sometimes with her head going side to side to follow his antics. If he gets too close, she swats with a soft fist, and keeps watching. If he pressed her too hard, she'd just go higher, but only a small percentage of the time does she run entirely out of his sight. Today they can go nose to nose to say hello, and even curl up across the bed from each other and stay out of each other's way. Toby's not a year old yet, so we're certain she's not through training him. She looks past his appearance, his clumsiness, and his size (55 pounds already) and sees the sweet puppy that just wants to play.

PATIENCE IS A VIRTUE, they say. It's not big news, but it may be the most difficult quality to master for the typical Type-A personality that tends to end up in leadership. Serenity doesn't come easily. The ability to be patient, and maybe, more importantly, to observe the behavior of our folks is extremely challenging for some, but it is critical. How can we coach and train if we don't watch? If we don't see the small changes that come as we share our hard won wisdom?

If we drive our charges away with claws out, sighs of impatience, rolling of eyeballs and exasperation in our voices, how can they see the right path to take on when, someday, we aren't there to guide them? If they see these small, but debilitating negative cues, will they tune us out? Will they keep coming to ask questions if they know they will hear that loud sigh and see the body language that scolds them for interrupting?

Remember the rules about visual, vocal, and verbal cues

here from Angel's chapter. Pearl spent 80% of the time with Toby relaxed, calmly sitting there without any hint of stress. She just participated quietly, waiting for him to understand.

Even worse than having them tune out is if we actually crack their self-esteem. My grandmother Jean taught special needs kids. She tutored them one at a time, in her home, and knew so much about how to instill confidence. Talk about patience! She really did understand how to help these kids find their way around a textbook, no matter how long it took. And she talked all the time about building up their self-esteem, coaching their parents in this so that the kids wouldn't give up. That's our job, too. As leaders, we need to find the ways to build up our people, not tear them down. We can do that, accidentally, if we don't watch our mannerisms.

Sure, once in a while, Pearl corrected really bad behavior, and it was a little funny to watch her tail expand to twice its size and lift high as she swatted fiercely and ran up the nearest cabinet or railing or countertop. Once, just once, Toby sent her running up a 50 foot pecan tree. She went up 40 feet easily. (Maybe there were bobcats at that golf course too.) Those corrections were necessary, so he'd learn in no uncertain terms which behavior was not going to be tolerated. And learn he did! Over just a few months, he found out that he could play, and bounce and even bark a bit, and she'd stay around. As long as he didn't touch her, she'd stay put.

We can run an employee up a tree figuratively, or we can learn to stay patient and not break the trust that we've spent so much time building up. The secret is to do it immediately like Pearl does! No waiting six months until the next review, and no sugar coating. Just sit them down, smile, and tell them what happened and why it can't happen again. Follow up with an email or appropriate documentation according to your human resources department. Be relaxed, and smile, and keep your claws in. They will learn and be inspired to keep trying, because they know you're going to keep helping them without breaking their spirit.

Pearl's beauty brought her home, but her patience is what makes her such a special part of the family. Your patience can make the difference to an employee that has spectacular potential that you may not see right at first, sort of like the beauty of Pearl's markings that I could not see from Facebook, but was amazing once we got her home.

For Avian Friends

Josie

Survival & Adaptation
How Did She Live to be 20?

JOSIE WAS THE MOST gorgeous bird I have ever seen. And I had the privilege of caring for her for two decades. She lived to be almost 20, longer than any cockatiel should live in captivity.

Josie taught me that we can survive beyond all expectations. She was a Christmas present, meant to be the mate of our other bird, Napoleon. In this case we did not get any baby birds. However, she outlived her mate by over a decade and was an inspiration to me.

First, she did not fall victim to the infection that took Napoleon too early. He was only seven.

Then, she survived a dog attack. She survived five moves: a move from Orlando to Tallahassee, nine weeks in a hotel sharing a small cage with two other birds (both of whom she also outlived), a move to the new house there, a move to a friend's house for a week before making a 16-hour drive to our rental house in Texas, and the move to the house where we live now.

Besides, cockatiels in captivity are only supposed to live 12-15 years. She died quietly overnight one summer at nearly 20 years old, and we buried her in the front garden.

Josie beat the odds because she had good DNA, excellent care, and attentive owners. We attended to the basic things, like fresh water daily and very high quality food, and simple, but consistent attention! We had a little routine with her–petting her head morning and night, talking to her, feeding at the same time daily, etc.–that didn't have to vary in all those wild circumstances she endured. Whenever we changed to a new cage, we even put the old toys in the new cage in the same places they had been before to be sure things felt familiar until she adjusted. This is what our research taught us, and we followed the instructions of the experts. That might be one of the lessons for this story: follow the instructions!

We only had Napoleon when we got Josie. Several more birds were added until we had six, and then back to three, then just Josie again. But by the time she was an only bird, we also had six dogs and six cats and two horses. So she was no longer free to roam the house as she once had been, for her own protection. Still, she got an upgraded cage and plenty of head scratching! Simple attention made a huge difference in her day, and she was not afraid to ask for it! Female cockatiels don't speak, but she would whistle and squawk. And if we would dare to walk by without so much as a hello, she let us know it!

Survival can come down to very basic things that build us up in the good times so that we have the strength to get through the tough times. Good food, hydration, rest, and physical exercise keep us healthy. Building a strong foundation under your business with basics such as documentation, job descriptions, SOPs, etc., can create a culture of doing the right things and paying attention to the many things that will keep us moving even in tough times.

This discipline will give us a way to keep the routine even when all hell is breaking lose around us. Don't mistake this for refusing to accept change when it is warranted. In fact, Josie's ability to accept all those changes was the reason she enjoyed so many years! The strong foundation we had built under her and the routine that she could count on day to day were the reasons she could accept the changes.

A favorite boss, Don Hanle, once said to me, "Always stick to the flight plan. Then we know where to look if you crash." He was speaking to me metaphorically as a traveling field rep in the days before cell phones. But the advice means something more. Having a plan and sticking to it can help your organization survive, just like keeping Josie on her routine all those years helped her.

Napoleon

Fearless Exploration
"Whattayadoin?"

SIZE CAN BE DECEPTIVE. Napoleon was a little cockatiel, just eight inches long (plus tail) and cute as the little orange button on his cheeks. We adopted him as a baby and he got his name almost instantly.

As soon as he got home, he wanted to always be with us. He didn't mind the height of my shoulder and wandered around with me as often as I would allow it. The name came when he managed to crawl down from the cage and started walking all over the house alone–even rooms where he'd never been!

He was fearless. He was also talkative. He talked to the TV, to people, to his mirrors, and to his mate. He only lived about six years, but he learned, "whattayadoing?" and "want a drink?" and a lot of basics like "hello" and "pretty bird," and he could call a dog with his whistle even though we didn't have one at the time. The Mexican hat dance was one of his whistles, too. Maybe the funniest moment was when he asked my ex, "Want a drink?" just at the moment he lifted a beer can to his lips. Or maybe the time I was hosting a trunk show at my house and just as I swirled around to demonstrate a skirt he let out a loud wolf whistle.

Napoleon lived a full life in six years. We had a screened porch out back and many long, warm days were spent running around it while I was gardening or relaxing after work. He was never afraid of anything or anyone, and he never seemed to run out of energy to go exploring.

EXPLORATION IS A NATURAL drive in human beings. If it weren't so, we wouldn't have bothered with cars and airplanes and oceangoing yachts. We'd have stayed right in our own little neck of the woods and made the most of whatever life was brought to us. But we didn't. We broke out at a hard run very early, and we never seem to stop wanting to see what is around the next corner.

It seems obvious to say that we have to do that in business. We have to move forward at all times, and explore the various options and ways to use technology and other tools to grow and challenge ourselves and remain relevant to our customers.

The human brain brings us these wonderful technologies and tools. Because of that, there is another exploration that should never stop, and it is more of an internal process for you and your charges.

Personal exploration is vital to our health as an organism, as a thinking entity, and as a leader. Brain research done in an effort to cure diseases such as Alzheimer's or due to injury or stroke have brought us a wealth of information about how the brain works and what we can do to improve our use of this mighty supercomputer we carry around. Nothing we have ever invented even comes close. If we consider even the use of artificial intelligence was designed and built using just about 11% of our own brain, imagine what we could do if we tapped into just 15%!

So how should we keep our brain firing on all cylinders? How do we aid our charges in the pursuit of logic and wisdom?

As a leader, you should not only allow and encourage such exploration, you should demonstrate and require it. Unfortunately, the training and education line in most corporate budgets is the first to go when times are tough. Lots of great authors have made the case for the pursuit of more and better education. Burrus talks about the need for real change in our school system, as does Buckingham.

What your charges need to see is that anything that they can do to stay sharp will be allowed. How can you allow them to explore the realm of opportunities to sharpen their knowledge without ruining their productivity levels?

One exploration should be attendance at trade association events related to your business. Allow them to participate at various levels, spreading the memberships around your team so that everyone has at least a little exposure. Don't allow simple attendance at the rubber chicken luncheons, though. If they aren't participating, joining committees, and volunteering to help, ask them why and find a way to involve them or find them another group. So much can be gained in personal growth by allowing them to work within other organizations like that. They learn about other personalities, working styles, and what leadership style or group dynamics will help them at your office.

Moreover, they will be thinking about different problems, literally firing new neurons in their brain and growing their ability to work through issues with new brain cells. This can't be understated. Our physical brains have been said to develop pathways that grow deeper and deeper and therefore more effective, but the caution is that other pathways also need to be developed. To learn more in-depth about learning and how this affects the brain, read *The Talent Code* by Daniel Coyle.

In sales teams, I've often recommended strong participation in at least three or four groups or associations: one related to the types of clients you are seeking, one related to an area of business or philanthropy that is interesting to the sales person, and one that is purely for fun. The first two are obvious. But why should your corporation support someone's membership in the Antique Car Club, Gardening Guild, or Dog Shows?

For the purpose of sales people, anything out in the community where they can demonstrate their ability and integrity and make friends who will talk about the product or service they provide is a way to build a book of business.

For everyone in the organization, all the way to the mailroom and the receptionist, the reasons to encourage participation in the fun group are the same as encouraging the business and trade associations. They will be solving different problems and building a different type relationship with others in that group than they do at work. They will engage a different part of their brain, exploring the outer realms of their own abilities. A keener sense of direction will develop for them and their perspective broadens.

Some will worry that they lose an employee because of their exposure to other possibilities. This is shortsighted. If you don't let them loose a bit, you'll lose them anyway. And if they aren't at their best, keenest self by way of some of this personal exploration, you could lose the whole company or project because you have dull, tired, uninspired thinking in your team.

Brain science is breaking the brain up into many parts and identifying exactly where we process many functions. You can study those, and you should. I'll just mention two generalities, the logical left brain and the creative right side.

Unless you are in the arts, your business probably lives in the logical left side of things. Numbers have to line up, spreadsheets are developed, and sales are tracked. Human resources laws have to be followed with careful documentation. So, like an old vinyl record that is played too often on just one side, or the way the driver's side seat wears out long before the passenger side, we have to work both sides of our brain to balance out our growth.

If you are in the arts, you may already know this. I find most artists are much more adept at balance, and recognize their own need to have someone with a left brain ability to help them manage their right-brained creativity in order to make a living in our culture.

This exploration into different areas by your team can make a difference in your bottom line because they get better at thinking. Their brains may even work better over time. Some studies have shown play to sharpen memory (chess club, online gaming, and more) and reduce the impact of dementia. Better problem solving usually means more efficiency and higher profits.

That's why the fun, playful, hobby-oriented activities should be supported or even required. If you help build a better human and a better brain, you're sure to end up with a better business. Don't be afraid. Explore the possibilities.

For the Cowboy in All of Us

Gabby

Routine
Kindness Counts

GABBY IS AN AMAZING study in survival. You may see a pattern here. My animals often barely escape death before they know me and then they seem to live forever.

Kendall Rose was living at our house after being in boarding situations most of her life (as far as we know). But all she had for companionship was our dogs. She got so used to them that she would lay down in the front yard of our country house and tuck her legs up under her the way the dogs do. I wasn't able to ride as much as I'd hoped, so we started casually looking for a companion for her. When a friend mentioned she know someone who was thinking of "sending their horse to the glue factory" for what she (correctly) thought was a stupid reason, I decided to go meet Gabby.

Apparently, the other four horses at Gabby's house didn't let him eat much. At his age, with a foot disorder, he wasn't able to graze much, either. So when I met him, he was skin and bones with a dull finish on his coat so bad that I couldn't really see his true coloring. The owners were very grateful I'd come to see him and brought him out into the yard. Gabby laid his big, beautiful, tired head on my shoulder, immediately claiming me as his. Gabby was 17 years old, or he may have been about 19. We'll never really know.

That weekend, the owners brought Gabby to me and we started some serious tender loving care. Top of the line food has always been a rule for my animals, and he couldn't get enough of it. I don't know if that horse had ever had a full stomach until he came to us. He had been a pacer pony, trained to always let the other horses win, and then given the least care of all the rest. It was a hard life, and horses feel the despondency of their situations. At my house, he learned about warmth and shelter and full bellies, and he responded beautifully. The nasty, patchy hair came out with lots of brushing and baths, and I found I had a gorgeous Chestnut gelding. As his weight came up, so did his energy. For a few years, he did so well that we went riding occasionally.

Then, one day, he just seemed a little skinnier. Not long after that, he seemed to be laying down more and more often. A call to the vet revealed a foot problem similar to bursitis. There was treatment, which we started immediately. After another few years, though, those dosages of medicine were causing more issues than they were solving and we were afraid we had run out of options for my big red horse. Without the medicine, his feet were too sore to graze, but with it his teeth were falling out!

Recounting his story to the owner of our feed store, she mentioned an herbal supplement called Stop the Pain. After a month of putting this magic liquid in his feed daily, he was completely weaned off the other meds and we were managing his pain. He received a second reprieve and lived an additional nine years!

Gabby had to endure the move to Texas, too. We brought him in the trailer with Kendall on a cold, wet day. It was a 16-hour drive and miserable the whole way. We had to stop every two hours to allow them to rest, since riding in a trailer is real work for a horse. Imagine if you had to stand in the back of the pickup truck while it was moving 60 miles an hour, even if you could use your hands, but you couldn't lay down or sit down. I had real concern because of Gabby's age. We took every possible precaution and he came through like a champ.

Then, about two years later, on the very day we were planning to move the horses from our rental house to the new house we bought three miles away, Kendall died unexpectedly and rather suddenly. When we returned from the Equine Hospital without her, Gabby really didn't want to go into the trailer. It took hours. Then he had to go to his new pasture and barn that he'd never seen, and without his beloved Kendall. It was a sad day for all of us. When we released him from the trailer, I just stood with him and he laid his head on my shoulder. When I had to go inside, he laid down right in the middle of the pasture, looking so forlorn and lost that I wept again.

So we created a new routine for Gabby that we rarely varied. Having decided that we were not adding any more horses to the herd, we had to become Gabby's herd. So, we made a strict routine for him of three visits a day. Morning feedings were much longer so that I could sit with him in the barn area and visit. It turns out that it was a great time for my daily devotional. Then, as soon as we got home from work while the dogs had a chance to go out and play, I sat with him for his evening meal. And, right before bed, we brought him a small sliced up apple for a treat. He would stand at the fence nearest the house every night waiting for that apple and his goodnight hug.

That routine worked well, and he adjusted, gained back the little weight he'd lost when we first moved, and started to show signs of life again. Then, he met Dancer.

At 31 years old, my horse had a much younger girlfriend. A friend was walking her horse around our country neighborhood on a regular basis and she brought her into my yard to meet Gabby. It was love at first sight. After a few months of this, we tried play dates. One play date was all it took for us to decide they needed to live together. Dancer had also lost her pasture mate about a year before and was showing signs of loneliness.

Most of the time now, Gabby is two blocks down my street. He and Dancer visit my smaller pasture sometimes when my friend is out of town, needs a break, or is fixing her fence. It's a perfect arrangement and a wonderfully unexpected solution for both our horses. Gabby had 35 happy years, and we were blessed to know him!

THERE ARE A LOT of lessons from Gabby.

First, ask for what you need. I was just asking casually about taking in a horse in need when a friend heard from a business acquaintance about Gabby. If I hadn't spoken up, I would have never known him. Talking about the things that you need for yourself or your firm to others can rarely harm you. You may not reveal every detail, but you can ask questions and tell stories about your situation. The solutions could come from anywhere.

Also, don't give up until you're sure you've tried every solution. I'd been counseled that we'd done "all that medicine can do" for Gabby. My vet wasn't wrong, he just hadn't ever heard of Stop the Pain. So again, by just talking about my situation to others in everyday conversations, I heard about this miracle solution that has added many years to the life of my horse.

Gabby also teaches us the value of kindness. He needed a loving hand, a warm voice on more than one occasion to get him through situations.

This led me to create an acronym for KIND leadership:

K is for Kind: Well, this one is obvious. Just breathe, think, and consider treating everyone the way you would a newcomer, the elderly, or a child. Aren't we naturally kind to strangers and babies? We naturally give them the benefit of the doubt and assume they are doing their best. And yet at work (and home, perhaps) we are not always so generous. Why not assume the best of our employees and co-workers? Why not be polite and friendly? Everyone deserves a little kindness.

I is for Instinct: Our first and most basic instinct is to survive at all costs. We can't change that part of our brain. We can, however, direct it. As managers, we must dismiss the notion of the leader as master and king. Humans are herd animals, and so if we allow ourselves to consider the survival of the herd as imperative to our own survival, it will help us come to the correct mental posture for kindness. We should take care of each other.

I can think of no better example than when there is a natural disaster. In most societies, provided it is not dominated by a criminal element, everyone pulls together to help one another. This is true around the world. The natural herd instinct would tell us that the best leader is the one who will sacrifice their own life or situation for that of their followers. The best coach will carry the water to their team if that is what is needed. They do not think such work is beneath them.

N is for Nurture: Nurturing is a long-term concept and

requires that we pay attention from the beginning to the end of the career cycle of our charges.

D is for Dare to Trust: Several of our stories have dealt with both giving and gaining trust. Trust is hard to earn and easy to lose. Treat it carefully.

Like with Josie, Gabby's next lesson is consistency. He needed a routine to get over the humps in life, and consistency in his care and medication. The fact that he had a rhythm he could count on helped him survive in the tough times.

Don't quit until you're really done! Gabby found "love" at the end of life because we, and he, were open to it. (Ask me sometime about my 73-year-old Grandma finding the love of her life.) Don't give up too early.

Kendall

Acceptance
Being Home is Enough

I DIDN'T GO LOOKING for Kendall, but she was the fulfillment of a dream I'd had since childhood. All I ever wanted was five acres and a horse, it seemed. I got the horse first and boarded her until the acreage was possible.

While visiting a friend's horse, we learned that there was a palomino mare that had been abandoned at the boarding facility. The proprietor was looking for someone to take her since he couldn't keep up with her expenses much longer. My friend and I split the cost and I later bought out her share of Kendall so she could get her own horse. This is one of those stories where all the stars aligned just right so it could work. By splitting the cost, and because my friend was a vet, we could both afford to do this.

I knew nothing about Kendall's situation, nor did the boarder who sold her to us. I had her checked out by the farrier and the vet and found all was well. But we didn't even know if she knew an English saddle or a western one. Since I had western, we just gave it a shot. She was never happy under the saddle, so we didn't ride a lot. Once we moved from central Florida to Tallahassee and had the acreage, I found a group of riders in the neighborhood and spent some time exploring the surrounding woods. It was a great time until both Kendall and I suffered minor injuries. By the time she recovered from her sprained tendon, I was having knee surgery (again). So we had only a short time as rider and horse.

That didn't change how much I cared for her, but on two occasions, once while we lived in Florida and once in Texas, I was very worried that she was unhappy just hanging around our pasture, even after we got Gabby there.

So, each time, I found a suitable home for her and we sent her to be with a larger group of horses and situations where she could have more attention and more time to be ridden and worked. Neither situation worked.

The first family had four kids and four other horses and Kendall just didn't fit in. We brought her home and she and Gabby had a nice reunion. She seemed fine for many years after that.

When we moved to Texas and had less than half the acreage, I thought I felt her getting restless. So we took her out to a therapy program for young children with disabilities. In less than a month they brought her home, slightly underweight and very happy to be back with us.

I finally figured out that what she wanted was to be home, with us. Our location or her levels of activity were not relevant to her. Of course, I couldn't just ask her what she wanted. In both cases we believed we were doing what was best for her, when really we were projecting our own feelings and assumptions.

Even when I couldn't ride, I spent hours in the barn or just standing in the pasture with my horses, brushing, hugging, and playing. Perhaps, because I would rather have been riding, I assumed the same for Kendall. But I was wrong. Being home was enough for her. She lived to be 20 (we think) and her life ended suddenly due to colic. We were happy to have her for 13 years.

THE LESSON FROM KENDALL is pretty straightforward. Don't make assumptions, and don't assume others need the same things that you need.

Listening well to the input of your staff is the key to not needing to assume anything. Just as many people don't know their own strengths, many will not know what they need if you don't help them think through the issues. As their leader, you'll need to walk some of your staff through the various scenarios, options, and consequences in order for them to work it through.

This means you have to remain neutral. Listening is a difficult, calculated, and strategic skill that you must study and develop. Hearing is an ability most are blessed to have at birth. Listening is a learned skill and we learned more about that with Jazz.

It's easy to project our own views, needs, and emotions onto others. Everyone wants to believe that they are right. Our opinions, whether due to the influence of our families, culture, or upbringing, become a part of us. Taking the time to study the facts surrounding the opinions we form is usually an afterthought, and as we see in the political arena, it is all too easy to find the science or theory we need to justify our position.

When you are dealing with a team member who needs to make a decision about their work, though, be careful that you don't have a personal agenda. Don't try to influence them too much to do what you'd do, or be like you. Doing this can have several negative ramifications.

First, it disempowers them. If you jump right in with your opinions, they may never take the time to go through the exercise of finding the answers themselves. This means they don't feel that they have anything to offer and that causes a domino effect. If they feel disenfranchised too often, they won't feel it matters much or how hard they work, or what solutions they bring to you. Read the classic "Who's Got the Monkey" article from Harvard Business Review.

Second, if they don't ever go through these exercises to find their own solutions, even if you do have to guide them, they don't learn much over time. You want to create independence, not dependence. You may have heard that you should constantly be training your own replacement. Your staff should be able to operate efficiently for long periods of time without you. If not, you're not training them well enough or delegating properly. Lead, but don't do everything for them.

Be careful, too, that you aren't hiring a lot of folks just like you. You need a variety of personality types, cultural input, and levels of education from various fields so that you gain a large number of different perspectives in your group. This ensures that you are looking at each project from a number of vantage points and that the natural ability and skill sets you have will bring any project to its fullest potential for success.

You also need other perspectives to help you keep your own emotional attachment from skewing the long-term view of your organization. If you have a lot of "yes men" around you, or people who have only seen the world from your viewpoint, you'll end up traveling a very narrow path. Broad options and abilities help keep you nimble in an ever changing world. You'll make smoother, quicker adjustments to the needs of your customers and your team if you can attack any problem from a variety of directions.

Projecting your own career needs can mislead you as well. Remember, one of our lessons with Caleb: everyone doesn't need the same reward you do, and not everyone even wants to be a leader. If you are reading this book, you have interest in leading. You want the role, and probably have at least some inborn talent for leadership. But not everyone desires it, and some avoid it studiously! So help your folks find their own path, and don't assume that any of your answers will line up with their needs. Advancement may not even be something they are looking for in their life. They could be quite happy right where they are already.

Sometimes, just being home is enough.

It came to me that every time
I lose a dog
They take a piece of my heart with them,
and every new dog who comes into my life
gifts me with a piece of their heart.
If I am blessed to live long enough
all the components of my heart
will be dog and
I will become as generous and loving as they are.
---anonymous

To see more photos of each pet in this book, visit:

www.TakingInStrays.com

ACKNOWLEDGMENTS

LIKE MOST AUTHORS, I am eternally grateful for the people in my life who have encouraged, pushed, prodded, and generally supported me in the long journey to publication. Without my church and pastors, my faith, and my God, none of my accomplishments, large or small, would be possible.

Dad, thanks for never expecting less than the best. You've been my rock forever. Mom, who taught me about networking before it was a business term, your natural sales skills came down in my DNA, too. John, you proved to me that no challenge is insurmountable. Al taught me to leave a legacy. My grandparents were all amazing in their ways, and each taught me lessons worth sharing (which just might be in my next book)! My extended family's support has kept me inspired. I love you all.

Sam Horn probably doesn't even know she influenced me so much at a Dallas area meeting of the National Speakers Association. Having seen her speak twice previously (thanks to Judy Gray, CEO on Call), I was inspired by her to draw and hang up the cover of my book long before I'd written the first word. Without that first step, who knows how long this might have taken? Thanks, Sam.

My friends Judy Hoberman and Kelly McDonald, also authors and speakers, have been amazing, casual, call-when-you-need-me kind of mentors and motivated me to just get it done. The best way I can thank them is to encourage you, my reader, to buy their books as well! Madelyn, thanks for listening.

I might have given up the dream a long time ago without my best bud, Kelly Kunst. No matter what stupidity I was going through, her friendship never wanes. Highs and lows for more years now than I can count have been weathered with her over the phone, over distance, over time. Howard and Kelly, love you lots.

There are lots of Pauls in my life. To Paul P., thanks for always believing in me. And Paul M., thanks for being my "on the job preacher" so many times.

I saved the the best for last–my husband. Paul, I have just one thing to say: I love you just a teeny, tiny bit.

About the Author

LISA HARRINGTON, CPCU, CRIS, CAM, AAI, AAIM, AAM, AIP is the Vice President of IRMI. She is a member of the IRMI executive team, and her departments are responsible for all aspects of marketing, conference management, client services and sales for all IRMI products and services. She has more than 30 years of experience in the American Agency System as a leader, author and trainer.

Ms. Harrington began her insurance career in 1983 and has served in a variety of roles, including educator, writer/editor, underwriter, sales agent, field rep, and agency operations manager. Before joining IRMI, Ms. Harrington was the COO and acting CEO for the Network of Vertafore Users (NetVU). She was founder and CEO of Sapphire Enterprises LLC, a management consulting firm specializing in insurance industry issues and keynote presentations for leadership, management, customer service and sales. Previously, she served as vice president of education for the Florida Association of Insurance Agents for 11 years.

Ms. Harrington holds a B.A. degree in management and Spanish from Ball State University and has carried several insurance designations and best practices certifications, including CPCU, CRIS, CAE, CAM, AAI, AAM, AIAP, and AIP.

Follow the author at:

www.twitter.com/crosslady62
www.TakingInStrays.com

If you enjoyed this book,
check out our other titles at

www.plaidforwomen.com